English Flowers and Gardens

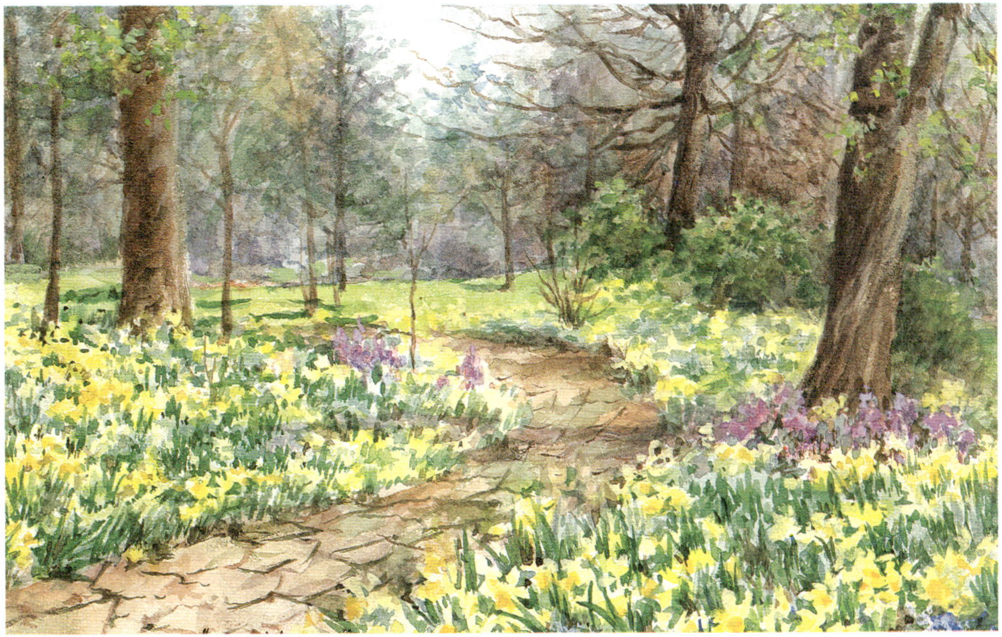

Flowers preach to us if we will hear
Christina G Rossetti

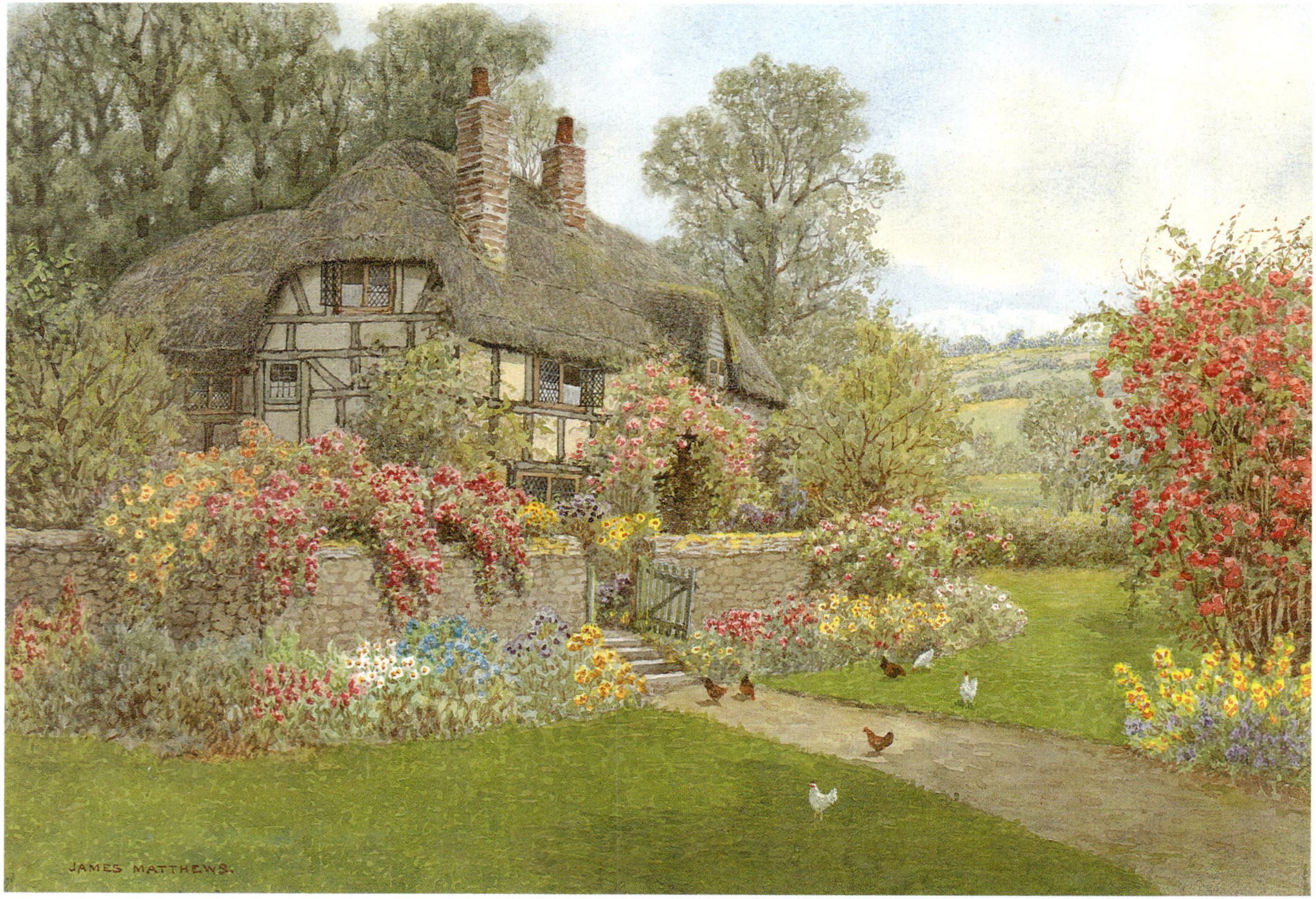

"Home, sweet home" by James Matthews

ENGLISH FLOWERS AND GARDENS

A golden treasury of floral gems

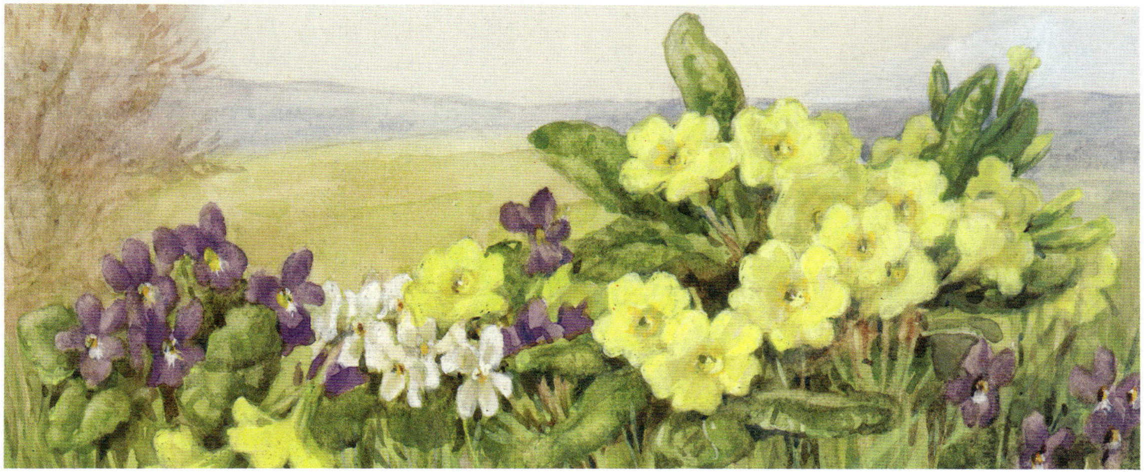

with the artists described and
with Gardening Notes by Fred Streeter, AHRHS, VMH
late Head Gardener, Petworth Park, Sussex

SALMON

Titles in this series;
English Flowers and Gardens
The Cottages and Countryside of England
The Rural England of A. R. Quinton
Countryside Companions
England's Pleasant Pastures

Published by J Salmon Limited
100 London Road, Sevenoaks, Kent TN13 1BB

First Edition 1992
Second Impression 1993

Designed by the Salmon Studio

Biographical information about Fred Streeter
by courtesy of the British Broadcasting Corporation

ISBN 0 906198 88 7

Printed in England by J Salmon Limited
Tubs Hill Works, 100 London Road, Sevenoaks, Kent TN13 1BB

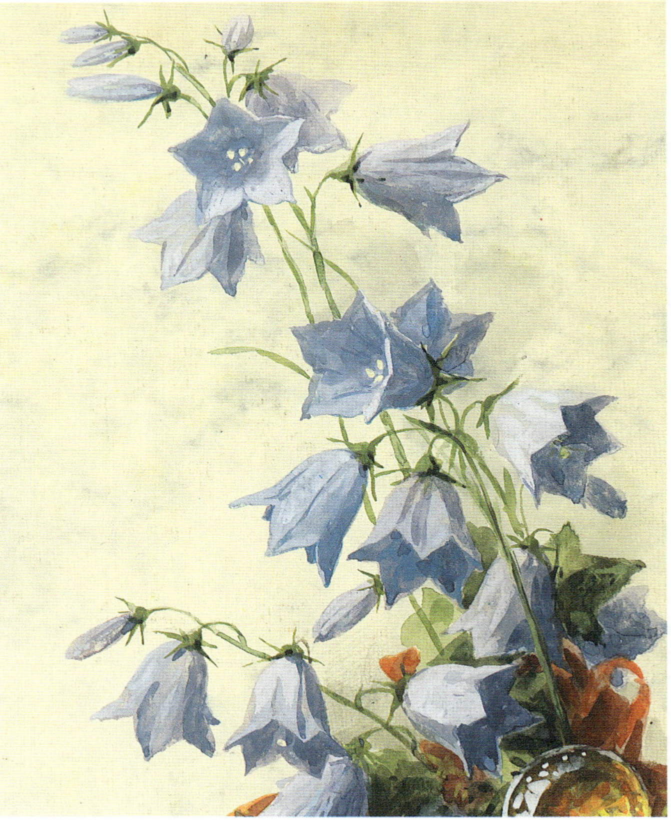

THIS INTRODUCTION is taken from The Encyclopaedia of Gardening, published in 1909, which was compiled and written by T W Sanders, FLS, FRHS, Editor of "Amateur Gardening" and "Farm and Garden" and Author of "The Alphabet of Gardening", "Amateur Greenhouse", "Vegetables and their Cultivation", "The Flower Garden".

THE art and craft of gardening is unquestionably the oldest of all human occupations. Holy Writ tells us that when the Great Architect of the universe created Adam, the progenitor of our race, He placed him in that delightful earthly paradise, the Garden of Eden, to dress and to keep it. We, therefore, who have adopted the noble profession as a means of existence have every reason to feel justly proud of belonging to so ancient and honourable a craft, while those who have adopted other professions, and who practise the art and craft as a recreative pursuit, cannot but share a similarly grateful appreciation of its virtues.

In the long vista of time that has passed since the first grand old gardener practised the art, first for pleasure, and afterwards as a means of subsistence, gardening has never failed to have a magic fascination for rich and poor of all ages. Noah, we are told, experienced delight in cultivating the vine; Jacob in growing the vine, fig, and almond; Solomon in making gardens, orchards, and vineyards; and the ancient Egyptians, Assyrians, Chinese, Greeks, and Romans, in the fashioning of gardens, or the cultivation of fruits and vegetables. In fact, throughout all ages and all time, the noble art and craft has ever been a popular and fascinating pursuit.

King Solomon must have been an enthusiastic amateur gardener, since he tells us in Ecclesiastes that, "I planted me vineyards: I made me gardens and orchards, and I planted trees in them of all kind of fruits: I made me pools of water, to water therewith the wood that bringeth forth trees." The gardens of that period were enclosed by walls or thick hedges to protect the crops from prowling beasts, and the crops grown therein were the vine, fig, pomegranate, walnut, almond, medlar, and quince; lettuce, endive, cucumbers, onions, leeks, garlic, and melons; and roses galore. In the hot, dry climate of Palestine watering was an indispensable operation, and hence reservoirs and conduits for irrigating the land had always to be provided.

In ancient Persia and Assyria gardens were fashioned and maintained on an elaborate style in the neighbourhood of all

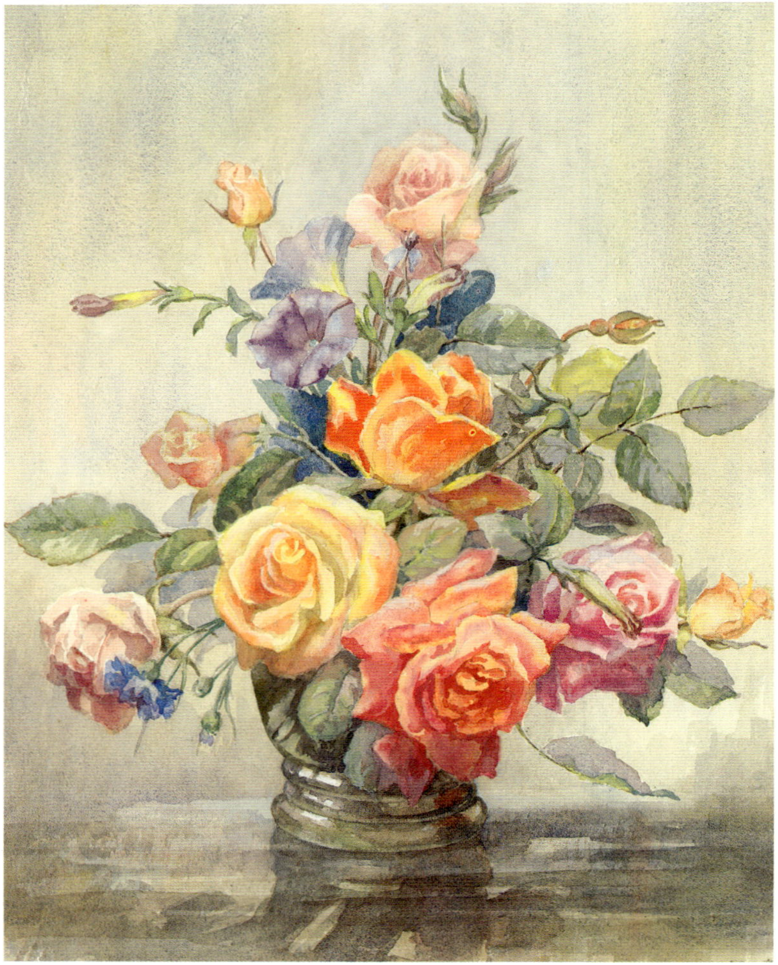

great cities. Not only were all the choicest of the native flora utilised in their adornment, but others obtained from far-off climes. The famous Hanging Gardens of Babylon were the wonder of the then civilised world. These consisted of no less than twenty plateaux, rising one above the other, and resting on walls 22 ft in thickness, and each planted with trees or other vegetation, kept in constant growth by artificial watering. In Egypt, too, gardens were elaborately fashioned, sculpture and masonry entering largely into their formation and decoration. In these they grew every kind of fruit, vegetables, and flowers, all of which had to be unceasingly watered by irrigation from the Nile, or by the hand of the slave.

The Grecians also were famous gardeners. They seem to have taken special delight in having fine expanses of beautiful greensward, studded with statuary and pavilions, and furnished with shady groves. Fruit trees were lavishly cultivated, and lilies, narcissi, and roses grown in profusion in these gardens. Not less magnificent and less regal in splendour were the Roman gardens. The Romans, indeed, were keen gardeners, and grew many of the popular vegetables of the present day with great success. Moreover, they fully understood the art of manuring and forcing, and may be said to have brought the arts of horticulture and agriculture to their highest perfection at that period of the world's history. In China, Mexico, and in India, too, gardening was a popular pastime with rich and poor long before the Christian era.

So far as our own country is concerned, there is little doubt that we owe the early introduction of horticulture, and its sister art agriculture, to the Romans. When they had finally subjugated the ancient Britons, and peace prevailed, history tells us that the Roman settlers planted vineyards and orchards of apples, pears, figs, mulberries, etc, as well as grew corn, not only for home use, but also for exportation. In the twelfth century it is recorded that vineyards flourished in the vale of Gloucester, apple orchards were plentiful in the fertile county of Worcester, market gardens existed at Fulham, and that gardens attached to the homes of the baron, yeoman, and hind were fairly common throughout England. But these gardens were not of the neat and symmetrical order of those of the present day. They were simple patches or enclosures within walls, planted with fruits, vegetables, and herbs. The monks of the Middle Ages were great gardeners. Their superior education, peaceful calling, and general habits fitted them to undertake the culture of produce in the curtilage of their monasteries. Moreover, they were in the habit of travelling a great deal, and had the opportunity of securing new or improved forms of produce to cultivate in their gardens.

It was in the reign of Edward III, that the art of gardening began to be seriously taken in hand. Britons then began to lay out their gardens on a more ornamental plan than before, and to cultivate plants for use and medicine more extensively. The first book on gardening, entitled "De Yeonomia de Housbrandia," by Walter de Henley, appeared in the 16th century, and others soon followed, including the quaint Thomas Tusser, who detailed the work of the garden and farm in pleasing rhyme. In Henry VIII's reign the gardens of Nonsuch and Hampton Court were laid out with regal splendour, and in Queen Bess's time the potato, tobacco, tea, and a number of other useful or ornamental plants and trees were introduced from foreign climes to enrich the gardens of the period.

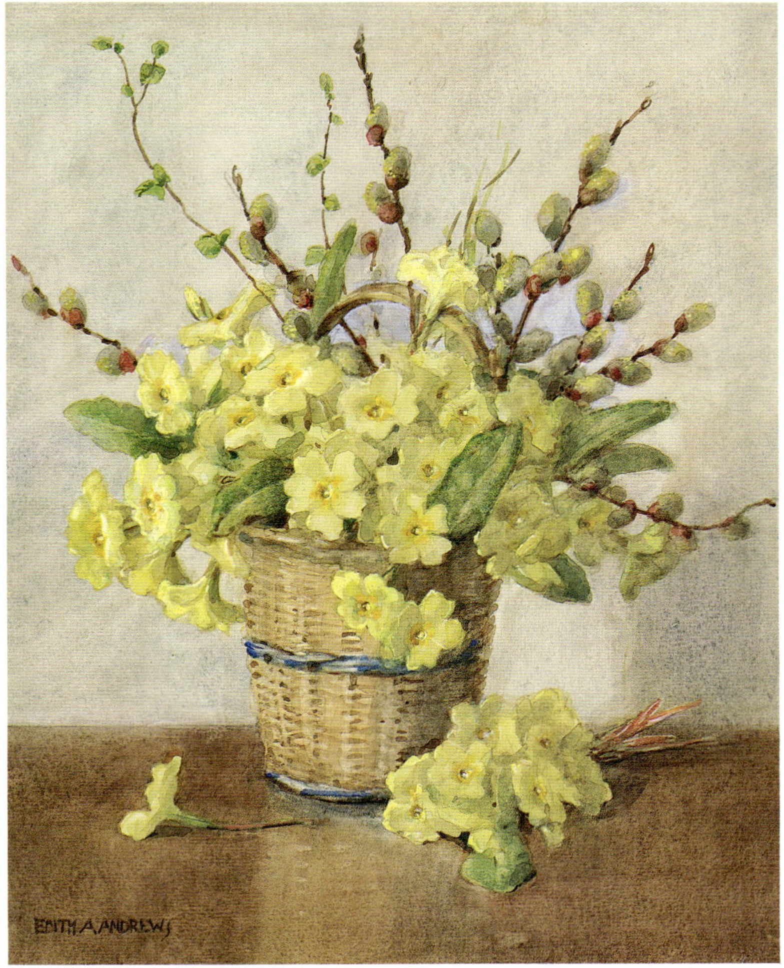

Evelyn, then a great writer and traveller, did a great deal to popularise and extend the art of gardening; and Gerard, the famous surgeon and botanist, published his esteemed Herbal, a work still highly valued at the present day. John Parkinson later on published his "Paradisi in sole Paradisus terestris," a valuable work, which gave great impetus to furthering the art of gardening at the time.

In the eighteenth century marvellous strides were made in the progress of gardening. People of wealth began to lay out gardens on a magnificent scale, form parks, and plant trees for ornament and use. Botanic gardens were formed at Chelsea, Cambridge, and Kew, and greenhouses glazed with glass and artificially heated were first brought into practical use at that period. The professional gardener of the 18th century was, however, woefully lacking in skill and intelligence. He could cultivate ordinary crops, but failed to possess the art or initiative of growing the choicer vegetables and fruit, hence these had to be imported from Holland and Flanders. Later, he seems to have improved, and to have been able to understand the art of securing early crops and ensuring successional supplies.

It was in the last century that gardening in all its phases made the most rapid strides, thanks to the efforts of such eminent experts as Thomas Andrew Knight, who did so much in the improvement of the varieties of our hardy fruits; John Claudius Loudon, in the designing and planting of gardens and in the publication of his remarkable Encyclopaedia of Gardening, and Trees and Shrubs, etc, both works showing a unique mental capacity and an amount of personal industry unequalled to the present time; Sir Joseph Paxton, the talented gardener and designer of the gardens of Chatsworth and the Crystal Palace; Charles Darwin, who rendered immeasurable service to botany and the improvement of plants by his researches and studies as to the origin of species; Dr Lindley, who did so much for us in regard to plant physiology and botany; and Dr Maxwell Masters, in regard to coniferae – all men of noble character, high ideals, and the widest scientific and practical attainments, who have, alas! gone to their well-earned rest, and left behind them records of greatness that will never die out so long as horticulture exists.

It would, indeed, be an impossible task to mention even a tithe of those, living or dead, who have, during the past century, done so much for the art of horticulture, either by pen or deed. The long period of peace which we have enjoyed, the more widely diffused education which has prevailed, the immense help which the plethora of societies has rendered, and the marvellous increase of literature on the subject, have all been conducive to extending a love of horticulture far and wide throughout the kingdom.

It may truly be said that there is hardly a house outside our congested cities that does not possess a garden, and even in towns where garden space does not exist, the love of gardening often stimulates the citizen to form a miniature garden on the roof, or to grow flowers on the window-sill.

As regards taste in gardening, a wonderful change has taken place in this respect during the last half century. Our own memories carry us back to forty years ago, and since that time we have witnessed a remarkable revolution, not only in the fashioning of gardens, but in the manner of planting, and the kinds of plants grown. For example, our earliest experience of

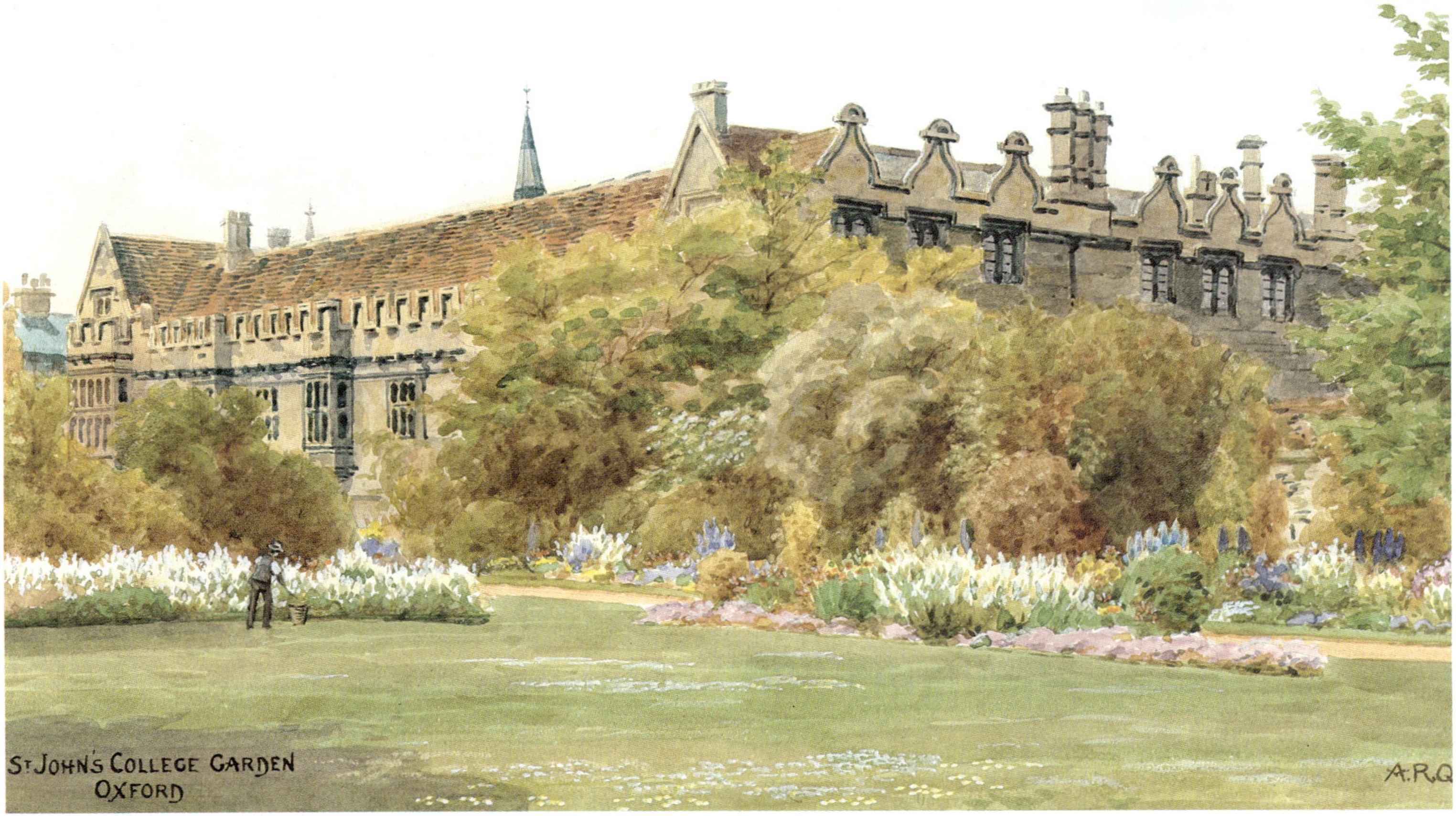

St John's College Garden, Oxford by A R Quinton

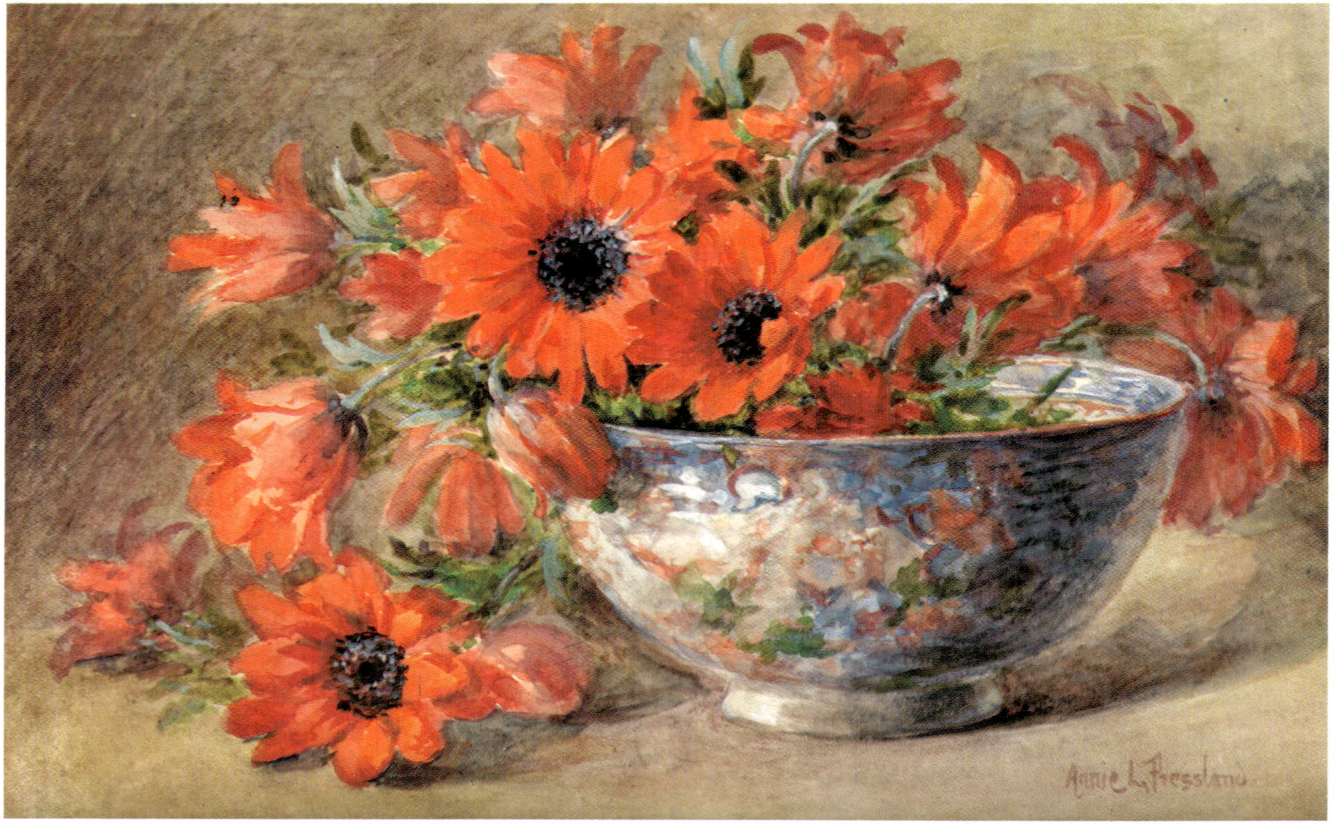

Anemone fulgens by Annie L Pressland

flower gardening was the strictly geometrical in design, and the planting of beds in a similarly rigid fashion – known as carpet bedding. In those days the flaring zonal, and the tricolored, bronze, golden, and silver-leaved pelargonium, the gaudy yellow calceolaria, and pyrethrum, and the brilliant blue lobelia, were the favoured plants for bedding, and hardy herbaceous plants and annuals were regarded as but of secondary importance. Every young gardener in those days regarded a knowledge of geometry as one of the essential accomplishments of his training, and many an hour was spent in devising intricate designs of a mosaic character for planting the beds the next season. Plants with beautiful or richly-coloured foliage were much in demand for filling in the designs, and any amount of labour and expense was incurred in endeavouring to produce elaborate and ornate designs in the way of carpet or mosaic bedding. This style soon satiated the palate of the wealthy, and then followed the even more costly range of subtropical bedding, plants of noble stature, richly-coloured foliage, or exquisite blossoms from tropical climes, being used extensively for decorating the flower garden. Eventually an apostle of nature came upon the scene, in the person of Mr William Robinson, a true natural artist, who fully appreciated the simple beauty and effectiveness of the wealth of hardy plants, and who unceasingly for forty years at least has urged upon owners of gardens the desirability of fashioning their gardens in a simple manner and more with regard to making them suitable homes for hardy plants, than as examples of geometrical art. Slowly the idea has gained favour with owners of gardens, with the result that to-day the strictly formal, hideous, gaudy, and repulsive style of garden decoration of forty years ago has given way to the more natural, simple, and truly artistic manner of transforming our gardens into pictures of natural beauty – the veritable reflex of Nature as seen in woodland, mead, or ravine. Thus, to-day, we see hardy flowering shrubs used to good effect in combination with evergreens, so as to make our shrubberies pictures of artistic beauty; our woodlands in spring carpeted with charming vernal blooming bulbs; the fringes of the lawn dotted with bold masses of golden daffodils; and our borders not planted with lines of gaudy geraniums, calceolarias, and lobelias as of yore, but with bold groups of hardy plants, that yield a continued succession of blossom from early spring to late autumn.

With the wealth of hardy trees, shrubs, plants and bulbs now at our disposal, it is indeed possible to have a garden beautiful in all its parts. We have kinds that revel in complete shade, in partial shade, and in full sun. The temperate regions of the world have, through the agency of the trade and travellers, furnished us with a remarkable wealth of vegetation for all our requirements, whether it be to plant a shrubbery, a rockery, a ravine, a dell, a border, or to clothe the walls of our dwellings. Thanks to the enterprise of our trade growers, it matters not what we require, we can get it, be it cheap or costly; every owner of a garden, indeed, has ample material to gratify his taste or meet the resources of his income.

> God Almighty first planted a garden: and,
> indeed it is the purest of human pleasures.
>
> *Francis Bacon*

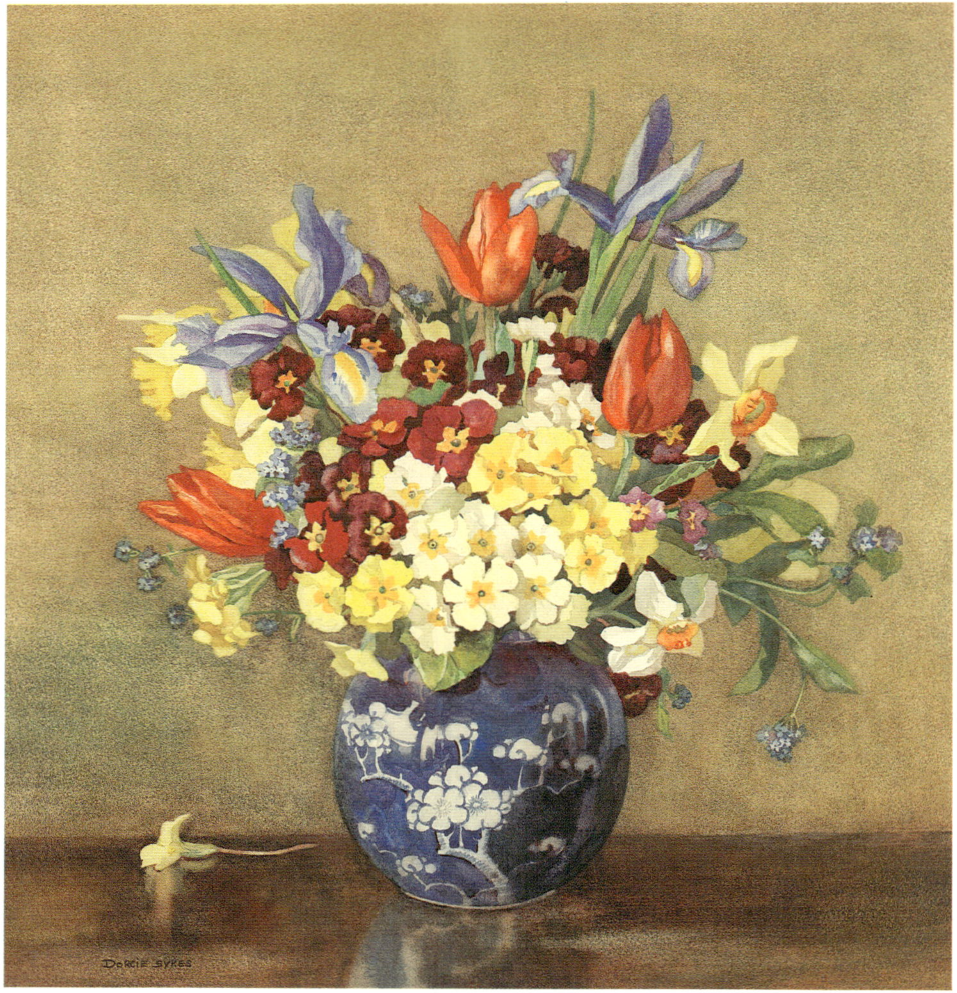

Ye bright Mosaics! that with
 storied beauty,
The floor of Nature's temple
 tesselate,
What numerous emblems of
 instructive duty
Your forms create!

Horace Smith

The Ginger Jar
by Dorcie Sykes

DORCIE SYKES was a watercolour flower and figure painter. A daughter of John Gutteridge Sykes, a landscape and marine painter who flourished between 1895 and 1936, she was born in Sheffield in 1908. She studied at the Harvey and Proctor School of Painting and began exhibiting at an early age in 1924, including the Royal Scottish Academy, the Royal Institute of Painters in Watercolour and the Walker Art Gallery Liverpool. She lived at 2 Church Lane, Newlyn, Cornwall.

Poppies by Dorcie Sykes

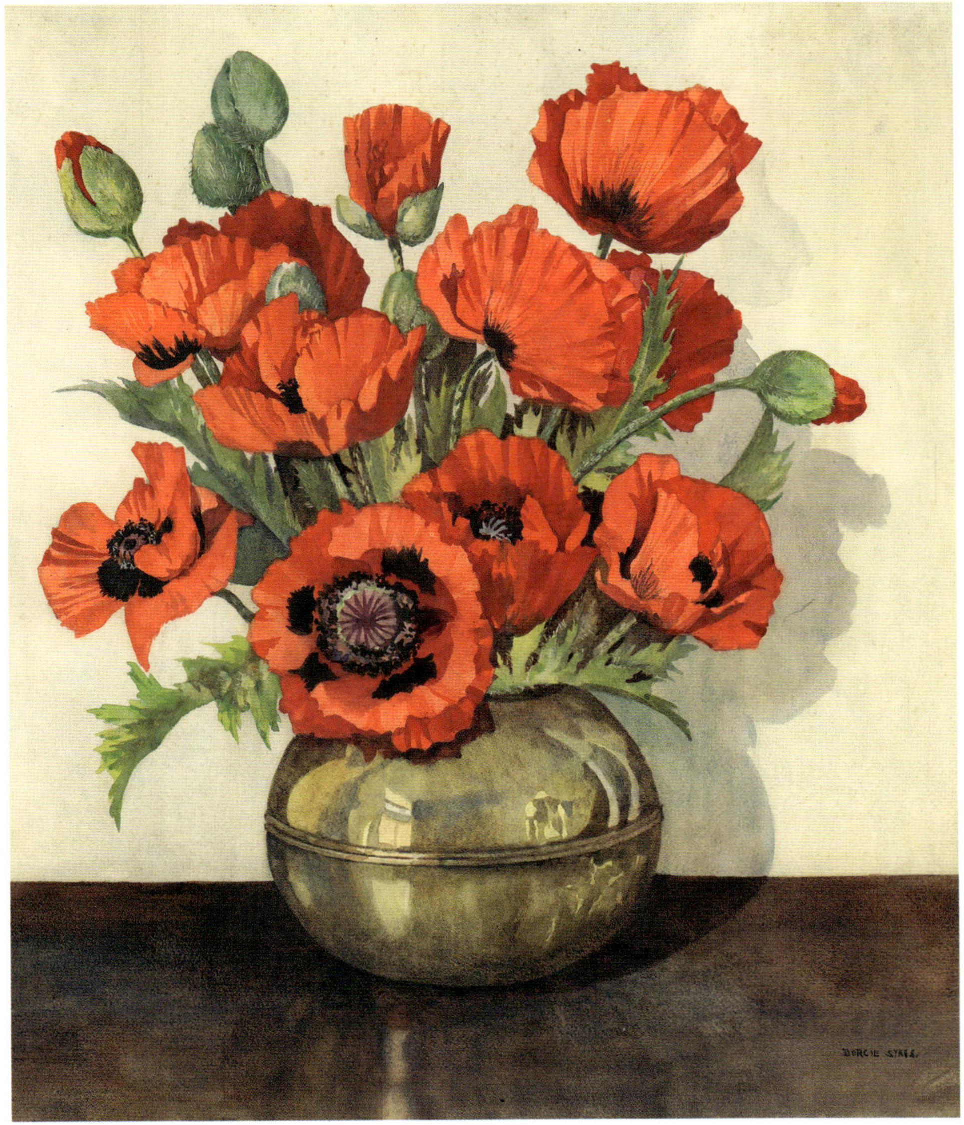

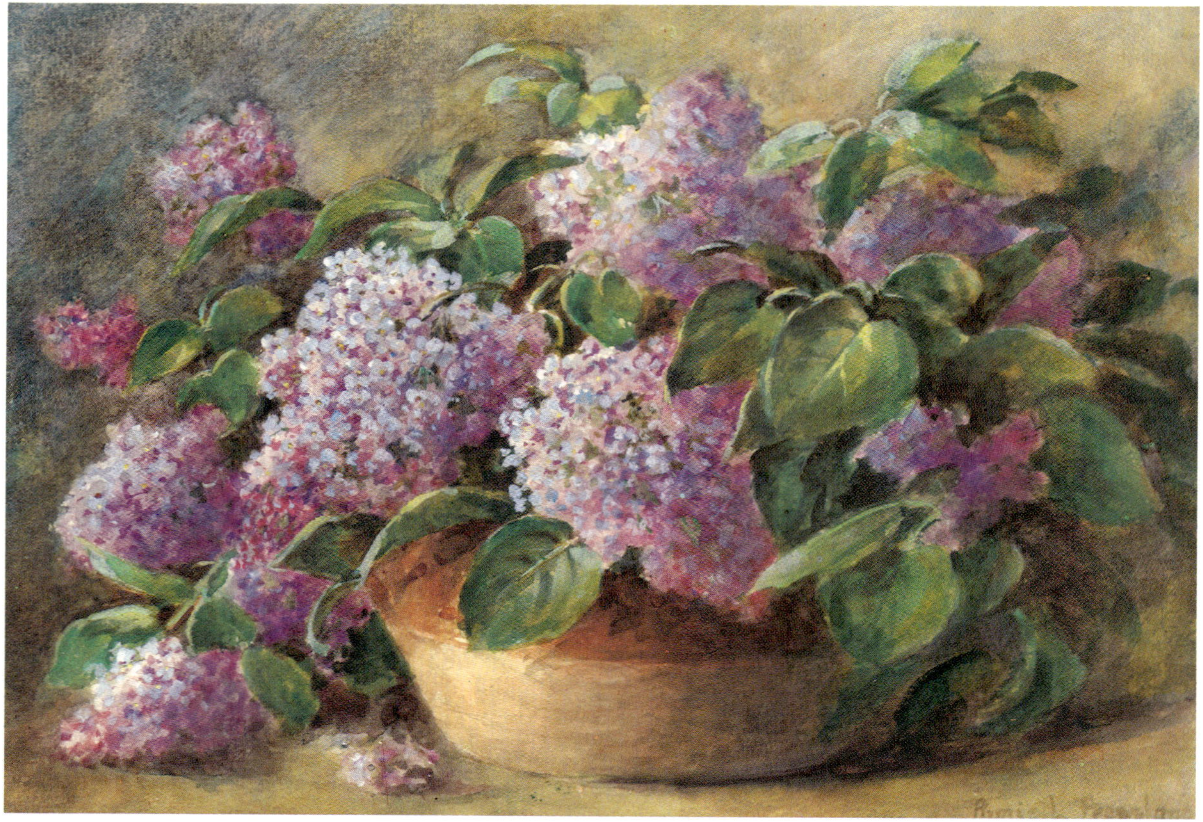

Lilac by Annie L Pressland

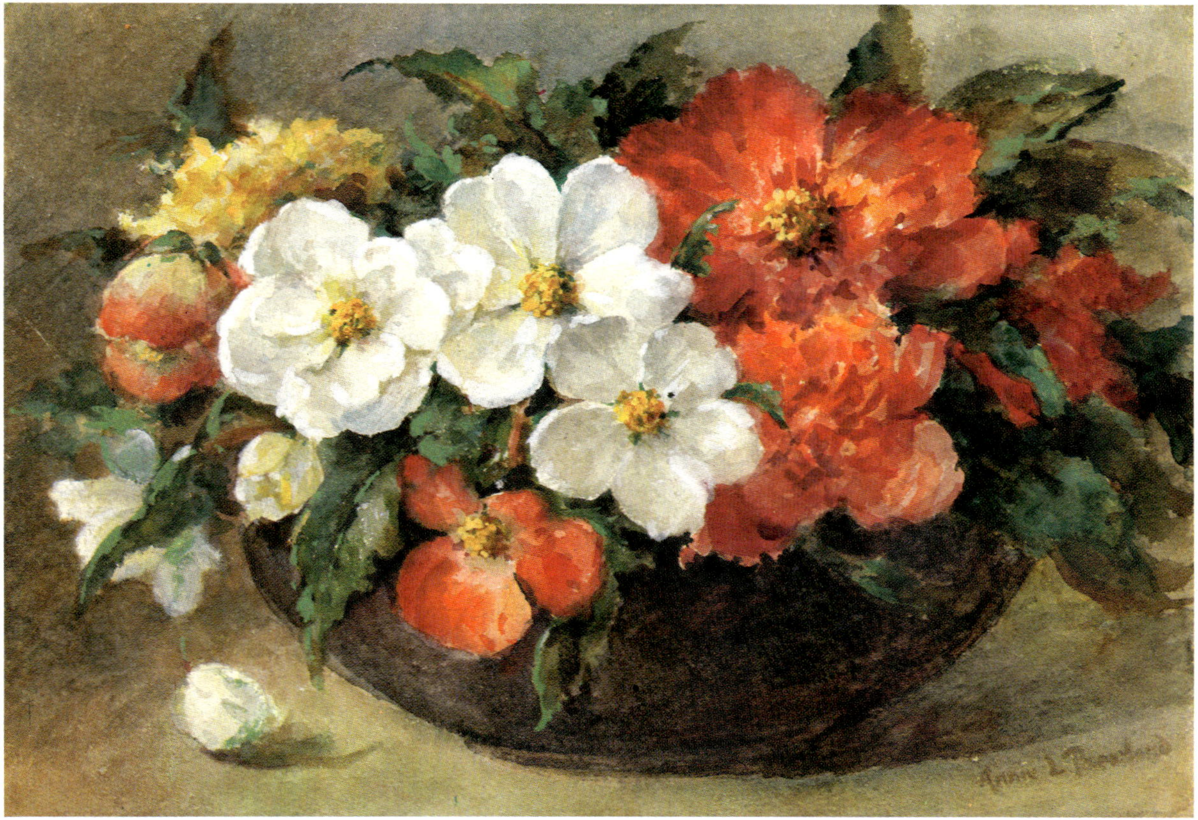

Begonias by Annie L Pressland

JANUARY

With the days beginning to lengthen, even in Winter it is surprising how quickly plant life responds. Bulbs are pushing through the soil. Snowdrops are even flowering, together with Aconites and the small Iris. The Erica Carnea with its pink blossom, winter flowering Pansies even peeping through the snow, together with several shrubs such as Mahonia Bealii, Daphne Mezereum, Nuttalia Cerasiformis, Hamamelis Mollis, and the Cydonias or Japonicas as they are commonly called. Even the Rhododendron "Christmas Glory" is making a brave show so who could say there is nothing interesting during January. Work of course must be guided by the weather. Never get on the ground when it is frozen or wet. During mild spells get your fruit tree pruning finished, also give the trees a tar-oil wash spray – always strictly to the directions on the cans. Get in your seeds from a reliable firm and always keep them dry and free from vermin. Make sure all tools are in good repair – never leave these jobs till they are required.

A Summer Morning by A de Breanski Jnr

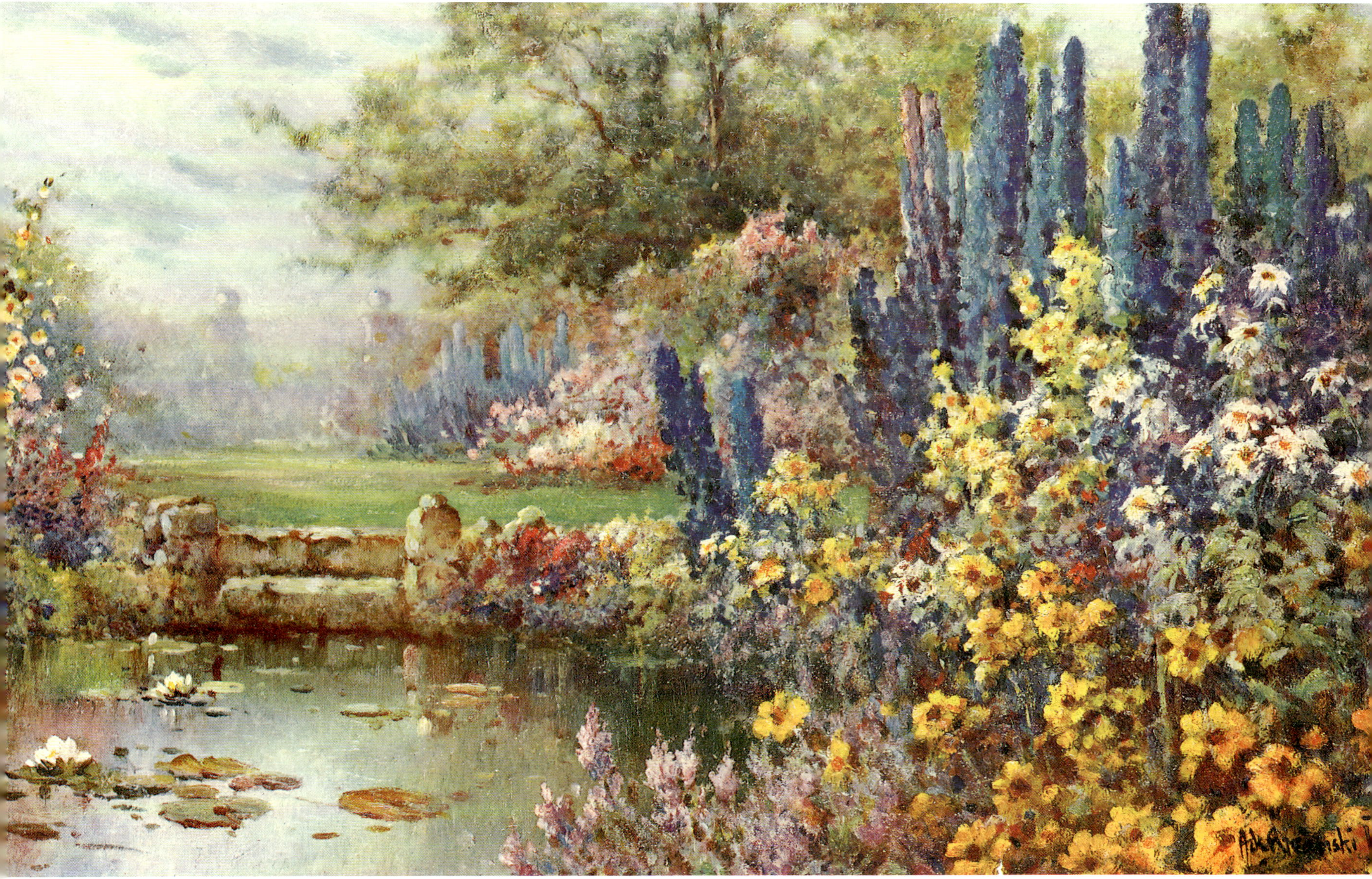

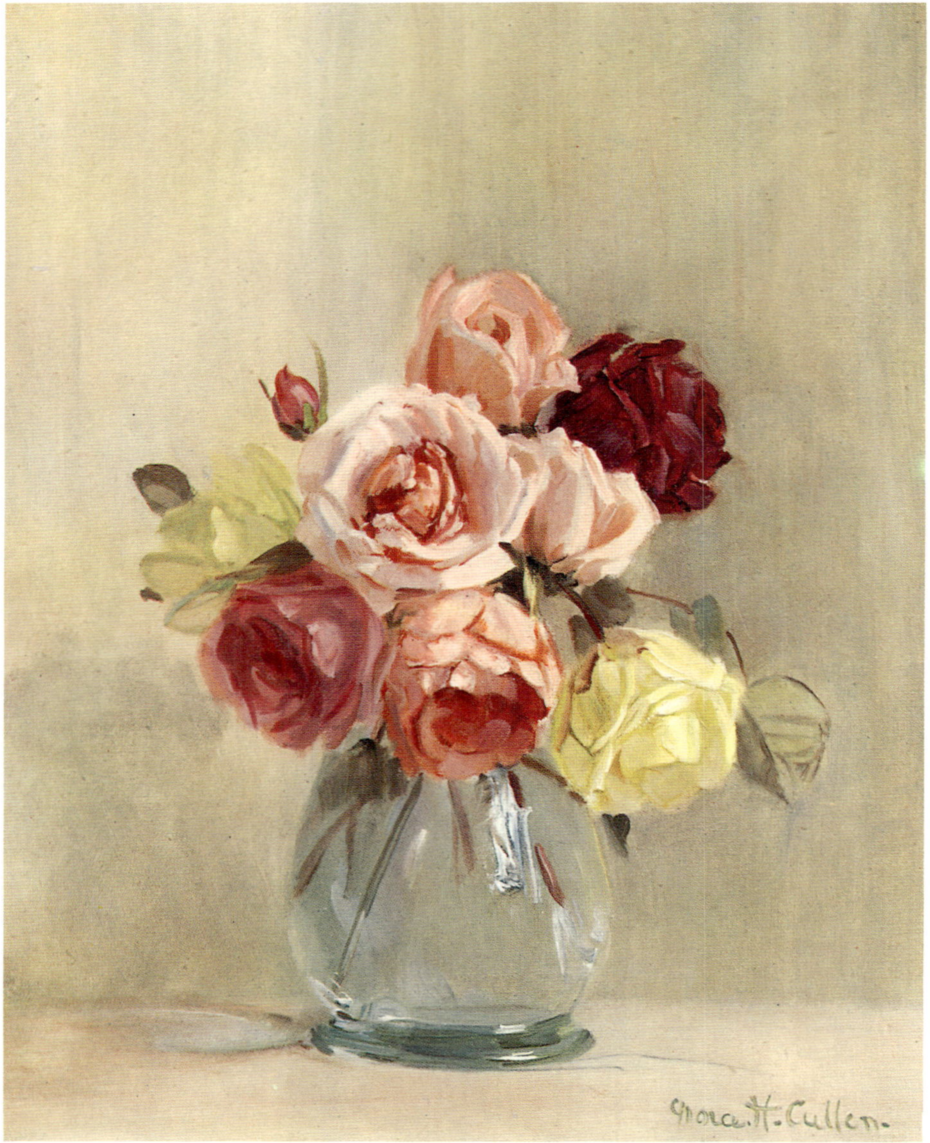

FREDERICK STREETER was born the son of a shepherd at Pulborough, West Sussex in June 1877. He left Reigate Grammar School at the age of twelve to take up a career in gardening. After a number of jobs in nurseries and private service he worked, for fourteen years, for the world-famous Chelsea nursery of James Veitch and Sons. After further service in private gardens he finally went to Petworth Park in 1929 as head gardener to Lord Leconfield. His broadcasting career began in the 1930s with a short talk on the B.B.C. on runner beans, which was an immediate success. Over the next forty years, in his rich Sussex voice, he shared his deep and abiding love of plants and gardening and the fruits of a lifetime's work and experience with millions of listeners; in 1945 the Royal Horticultural Society awarded him the Victoria Medal of Honour. He died, aged 98, on 1st November 1975.

A Jug of Roses
by Nora H Cullen

NORA H CULLEN was a flower painter, mainly in oils, who specialised particularly in roses and mixed flowers in vases. She exhibited, mainly between 1933 and 1940, at the Royal Academy, the Royal Society of British Artists, the Royal Institute of Oil Painters, the Society of Women Artists and other London and provincial galleries. She was married to Mr J B Cullen, a member of the grocery retailing family and lived at Cross Keys House, Sevenoaks until 1947 when she moved to Blackdown House, Crewkerne, Somerset. She died in 1949.

Springtime by Nora H Cullen

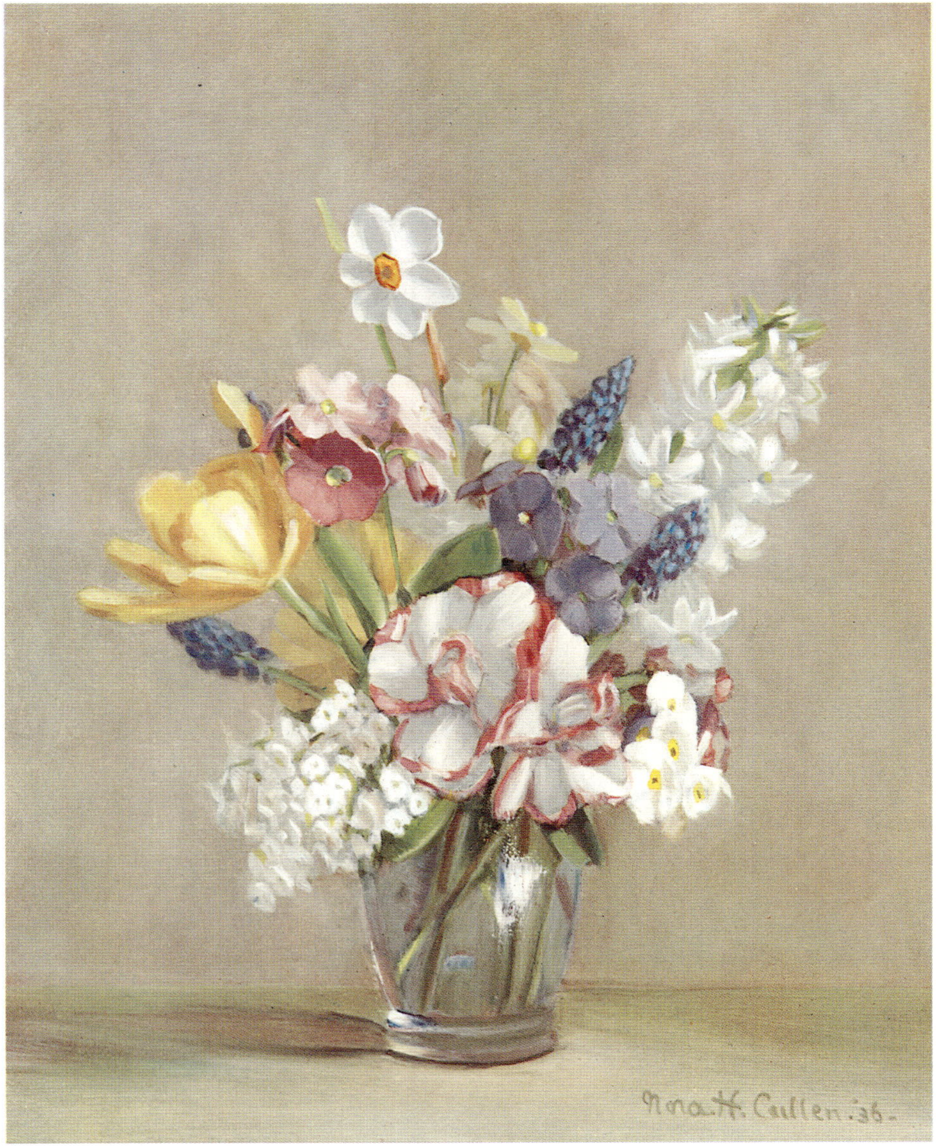

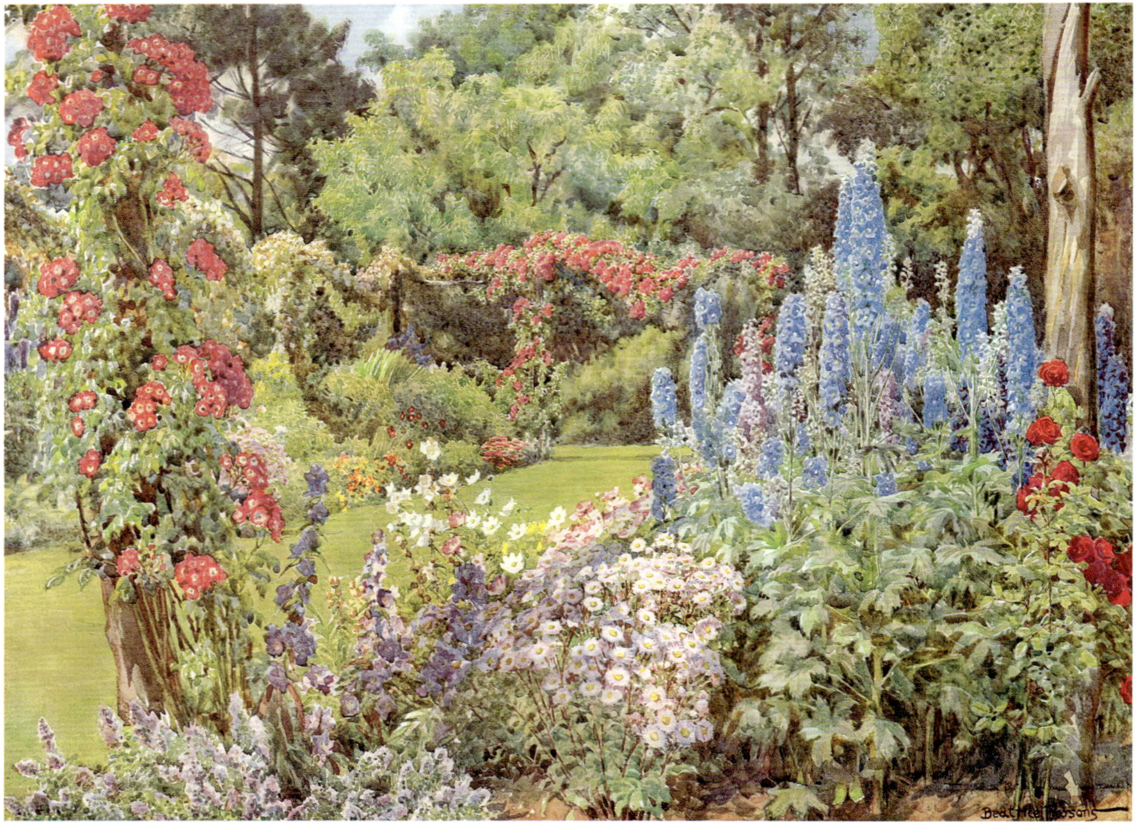

Midsummer Glory by Beatrice Parsons

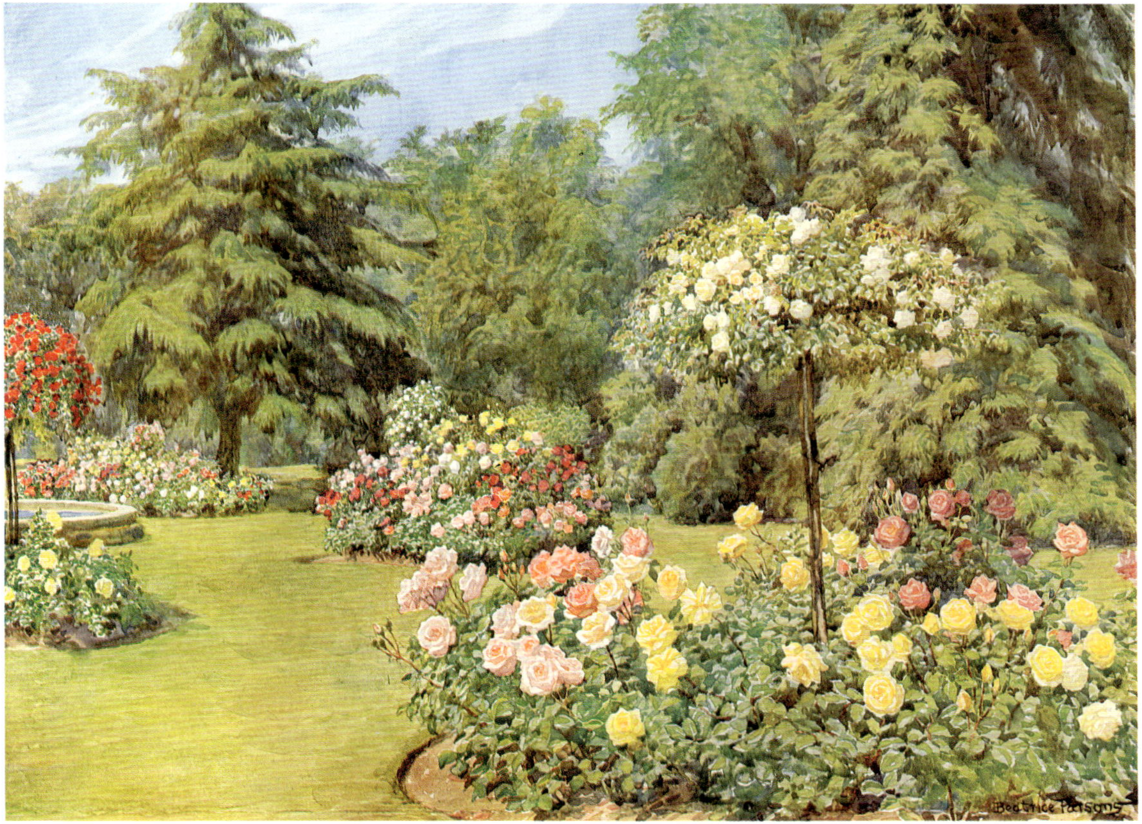

The Rose Garden by Beatrice Parsons

FEBRUARY

The busy season is close upon us. The rockery is fast coming into its own, different flowers opening almost every day. It's a good plan to freshen the surface soil round these little alpines and give them a top dressing with peat and sand or leaf soil; helps them a lot. Bulbs are springing up all over the place. The first odd Crocus flowering with fine promise as soon as the sun helps them along. When you are picking the flowers from the bulbs don't pull off the foliage will you. Never worry if there is a fall of snow; cold east winds will do far more damage. Spray your Peach trees with Bordeaux Mixture to prevent leaf curl and the Blackcurrants with Lime Sulphur should they suffer from big bud. To prevent birds taking the Gooseberry buds spray with 4 ozs of powdered Alum to a gallon of soft water. Plant Shallots and Garlic. Set up the early Potatoes to sprout in boxes. Push on with any late planting of trees, shrubs, fruit trees or creepers. Cut back hard any Ivy growing on the house and Clematis except the Montana group; the kinds that flower on the last year's growth.

Fred Streeter

A Sunny Home by H J Sylvester Stannard, RBA

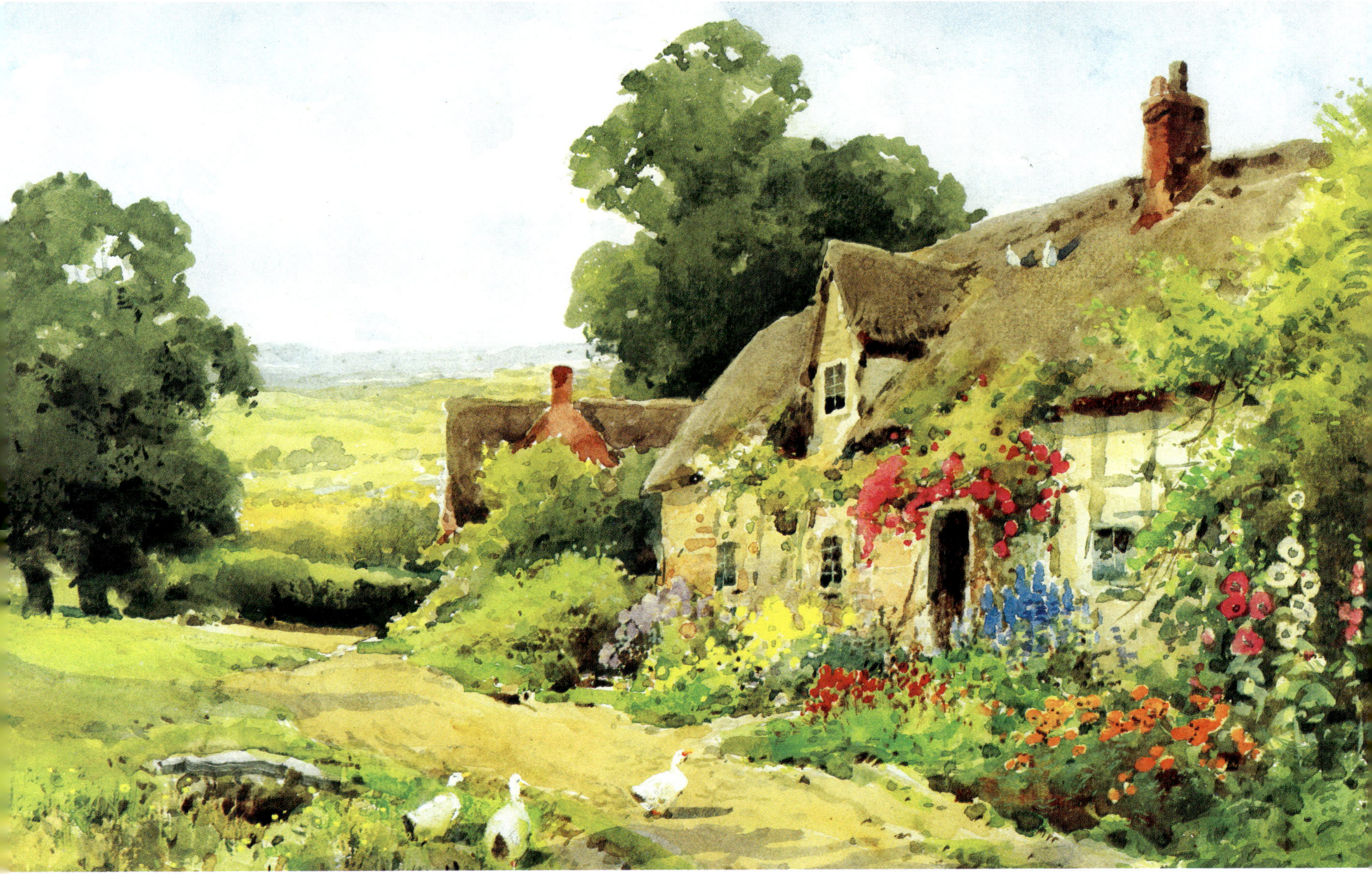

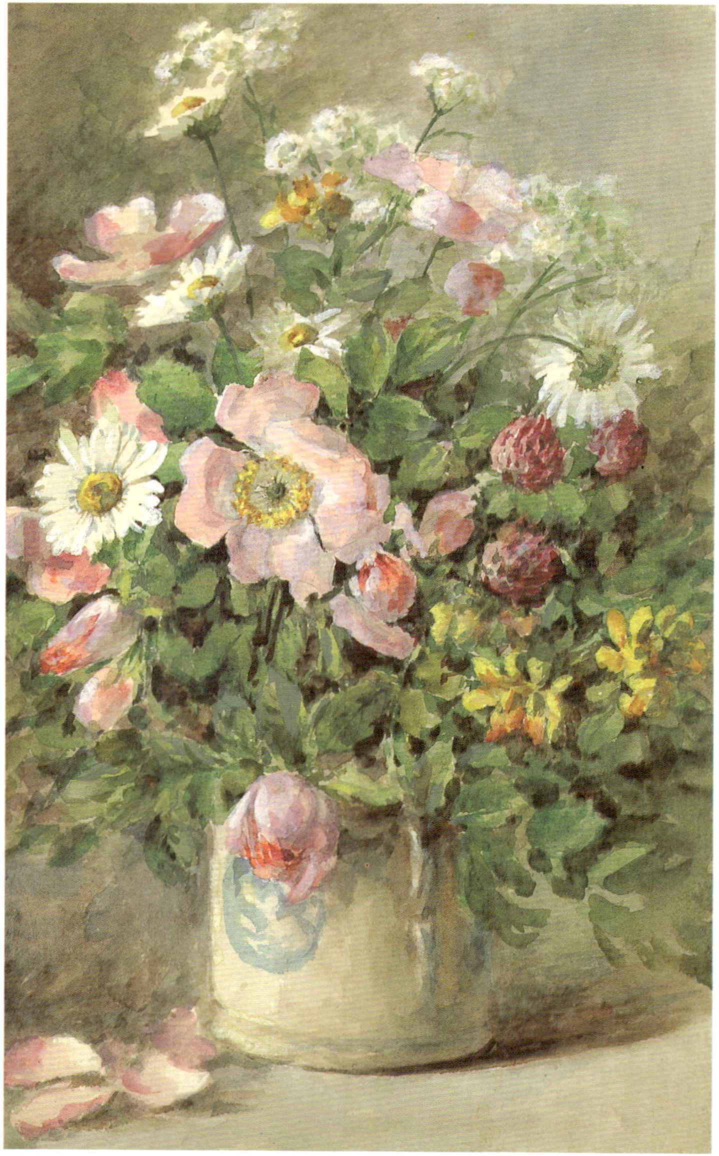

BEATRICE PARSONS was originally a painter of religious subjects but later turned to old-English garden pictures in watercolour and it is for these she is best known. Born at Peckham in 1870 she studied at the Royal Academy Schools and exhibited religious subjects at the Royal Academy between 1889 and 1899. In 1904, at the suggestion of Mr Dowdeswell, she held an exhibition of forty-four watercolour paintings of gardens at the Dowdeswell Gallery, Bond Street, London. This was an instant success and her reputation as a garden painter was assured. She travelled extensively in England and on the Continent, painting gardens for a wide clientele and exhibiting at London and provincial galleries, most particularly the Dowdeswell Gallery. Her paintings were executed in a strong, decisive style, full of colour and her flowers were always well drawn and individually recognisable. From 1907 she lived with one of her sisters at Oxhey, Hertfordshire, where she died in 1955.

Wild Roses and Daisies
by Annie L Pressland

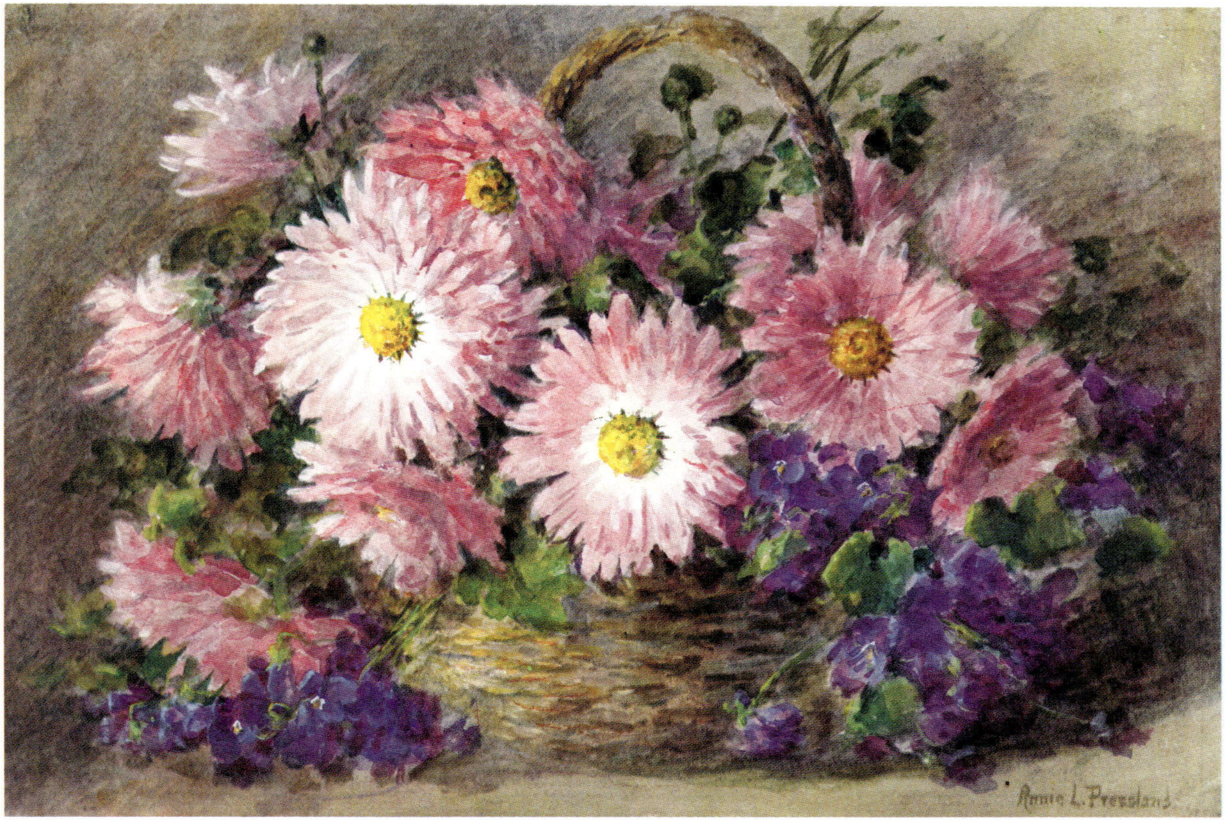

Single pink Chrysanthemums and Violets by Annie L Pressland

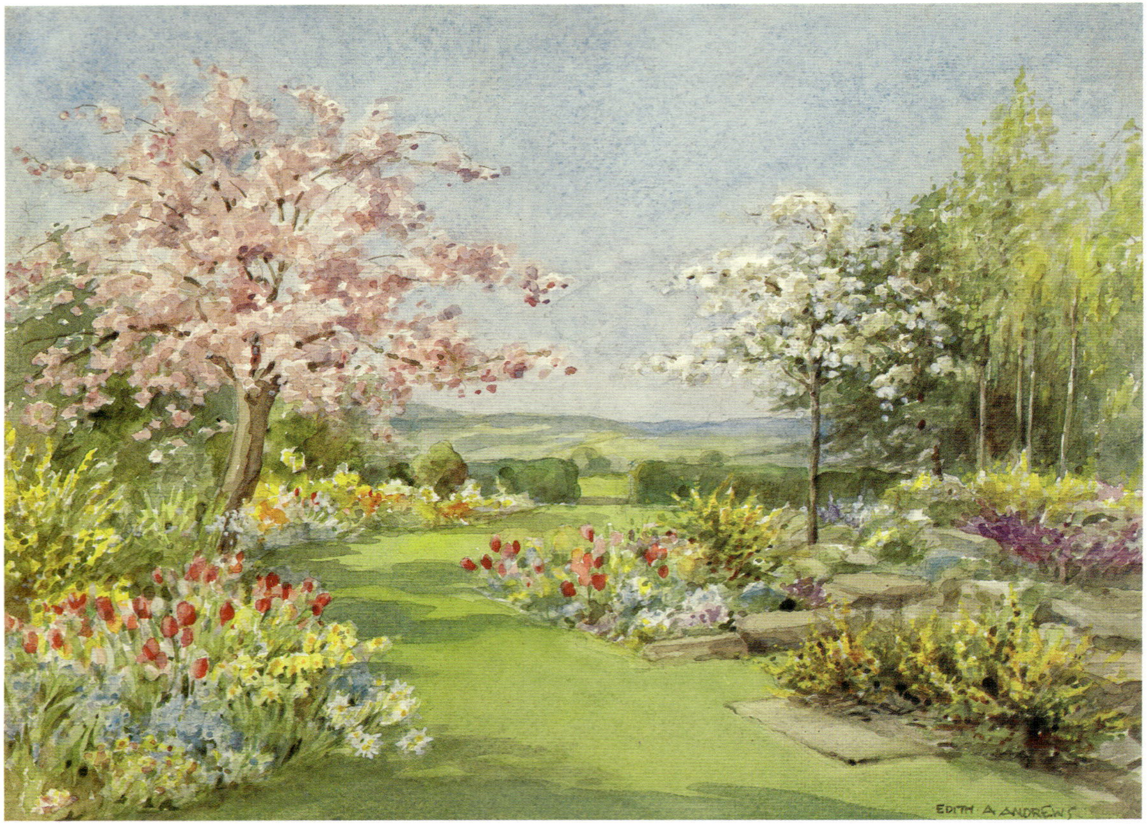

Bounteous May by Edith A Andrews

Sweet May hath come to love us,
Flowers, trees, their blossoms don;
And through the blue heavens
　　above us
The very clouds move on.

Heinriche Heine

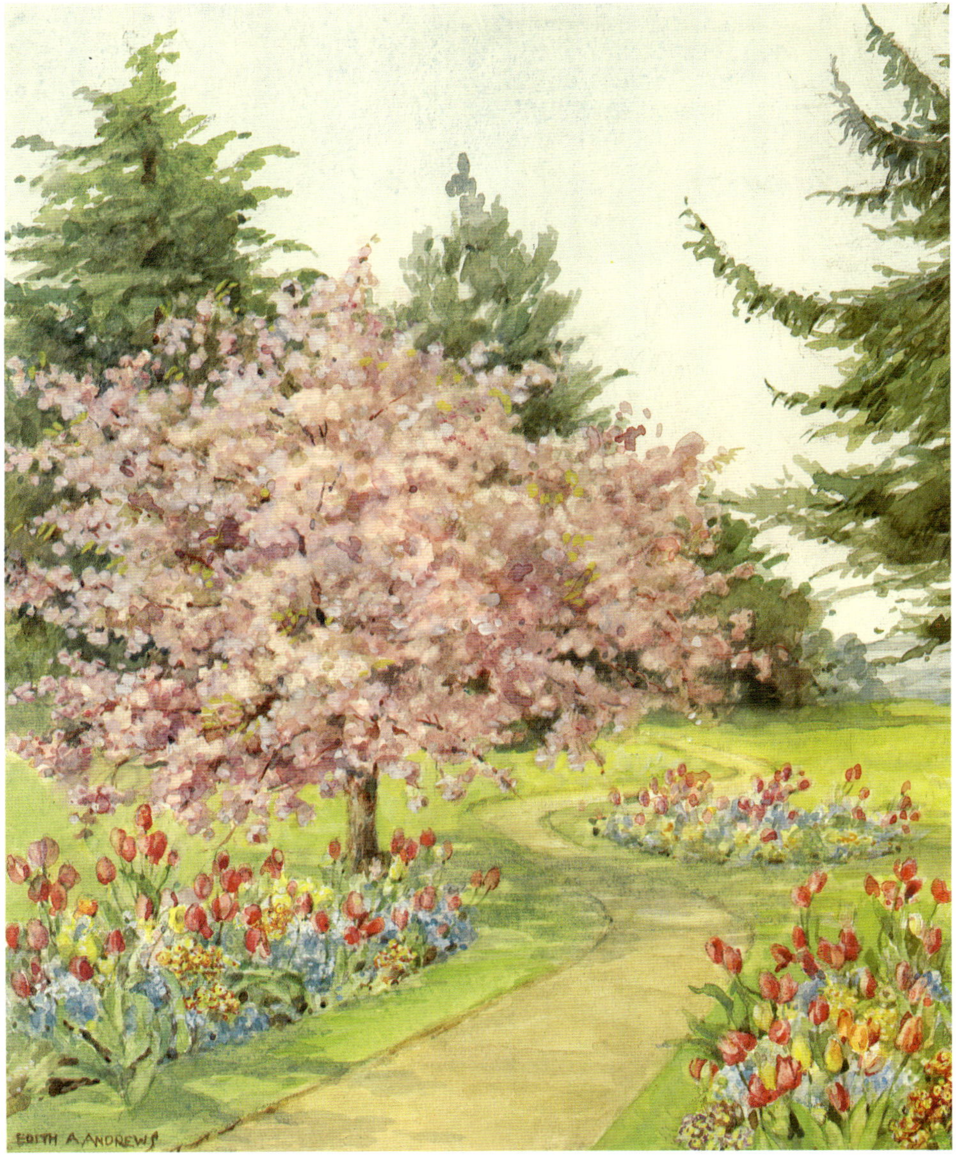

The Cherry Tree
by Edith A Andrews

MARCH

Gardening really does start now, but do not get impatient if the weather is unkind; wait for it and get the soil kind. The flower borders will require attention. Divide your Michaelmas Daisies; never allow them to get old and straggly. Take the outside growths for replanting and destroy the old centres and grow the better varieties. Fork lightly between the groups of plants and fill up blank spaces with annuals; these are cheap and lovely things for making up. Prune your Roses. Don't be afraid to cut them fairly hard – except Peace, which only requires tipping like the floribunda types. Sweep and roll the lawn when it's dry and run the mowing machine over with the knife set high. Plant out Sweet Peas on prepared ground; allow these plenty of room. Sow Peas, Broad Beans, Onions, Carrots, Parsnips, Lettuce and Turnips. Clean the Asparagus bed, raking the surface fine and edging the side of the bed; plant new beds and also put the herbs in order. Still time for very late planting but try and finish off quickly. Prune the Gooseberries and Red Currants and trim and clean the Strawberry bed.

Yardley Court Pond, Kent by Edith A Andrews

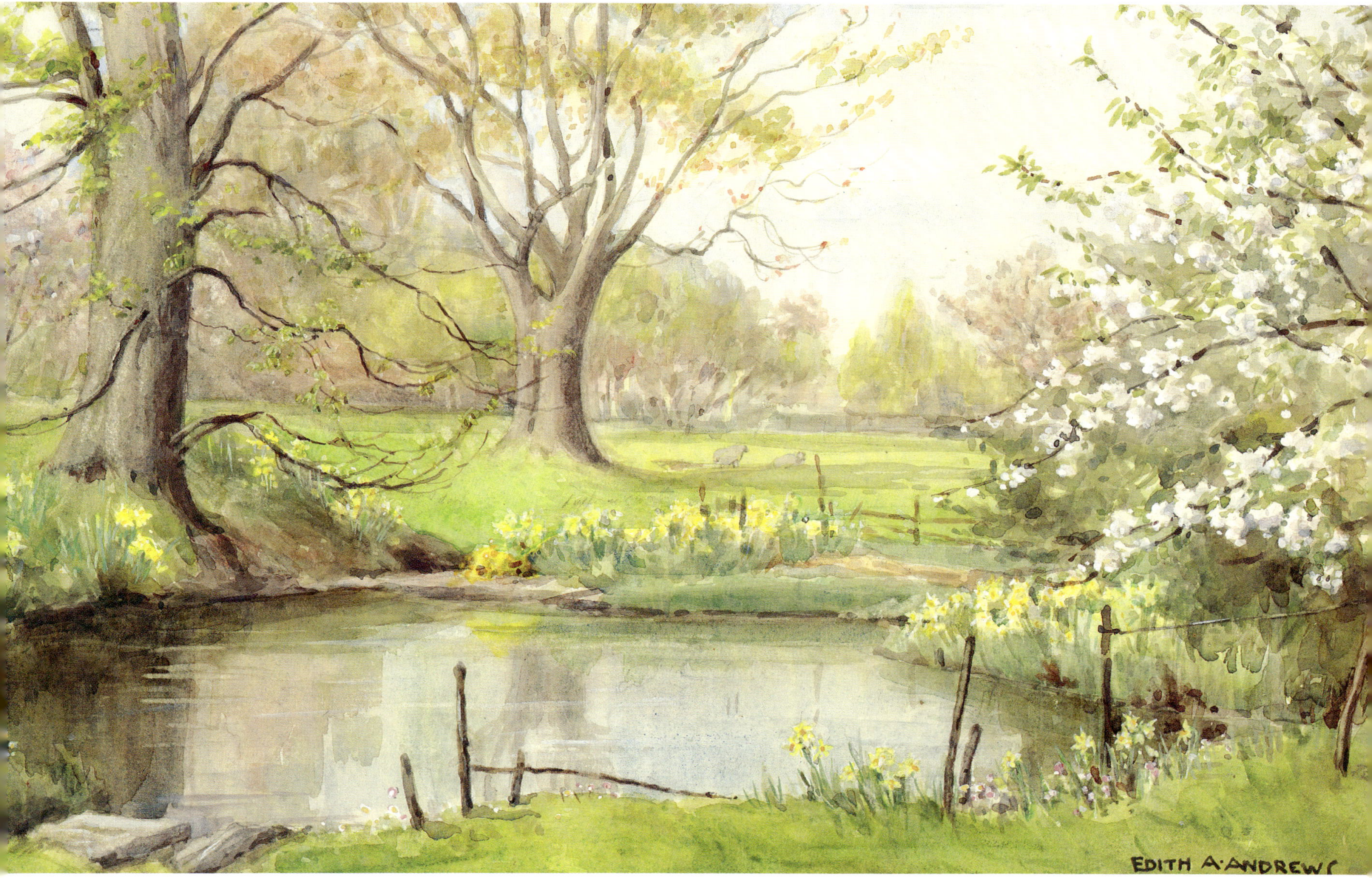
EDITH A·ANDREWS

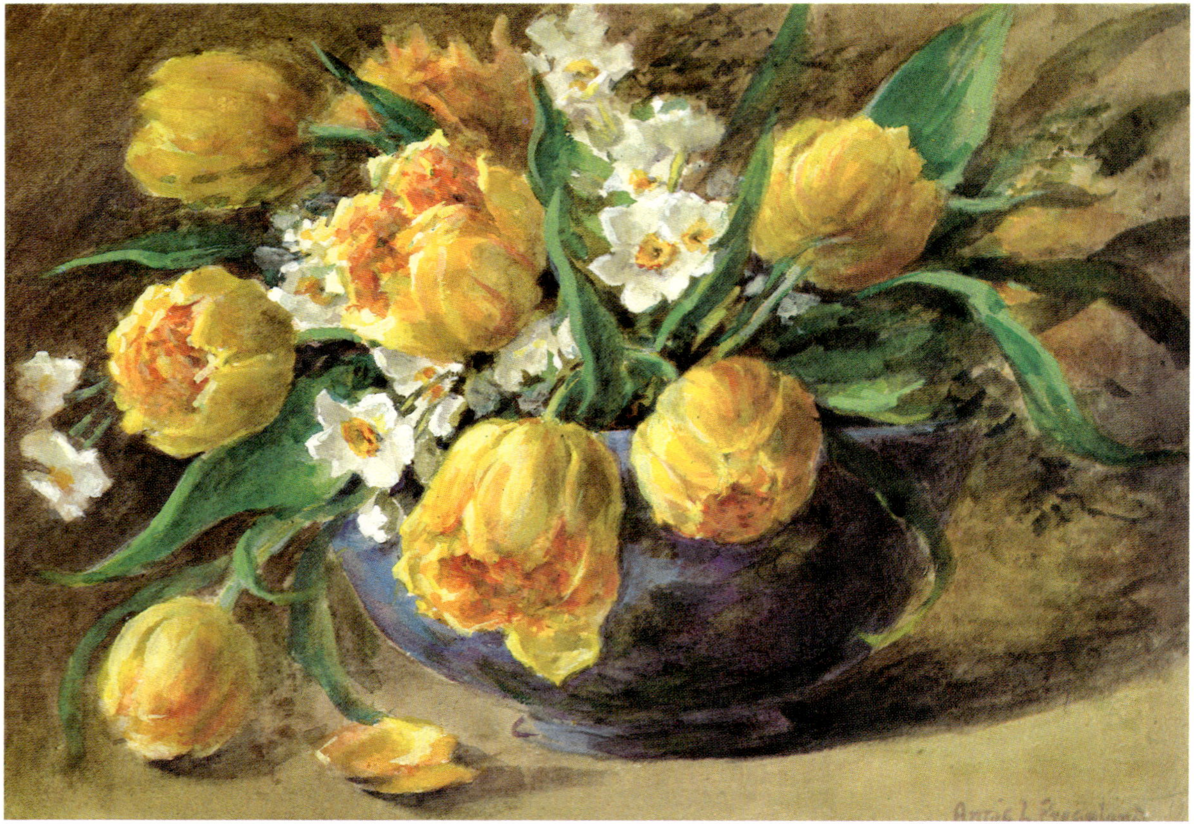

Yellow Tulips and Jonquils by Annie L Pressland

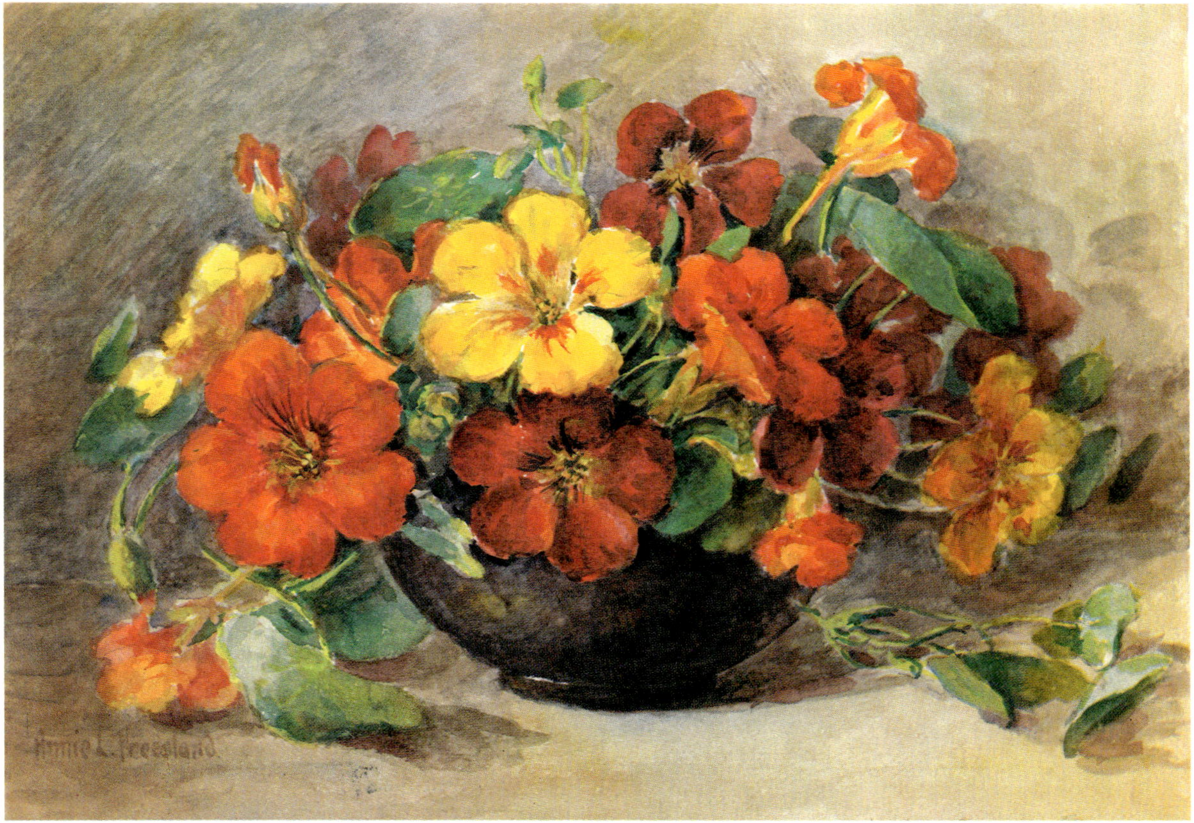

Nasturtiums by Annie L Pressland

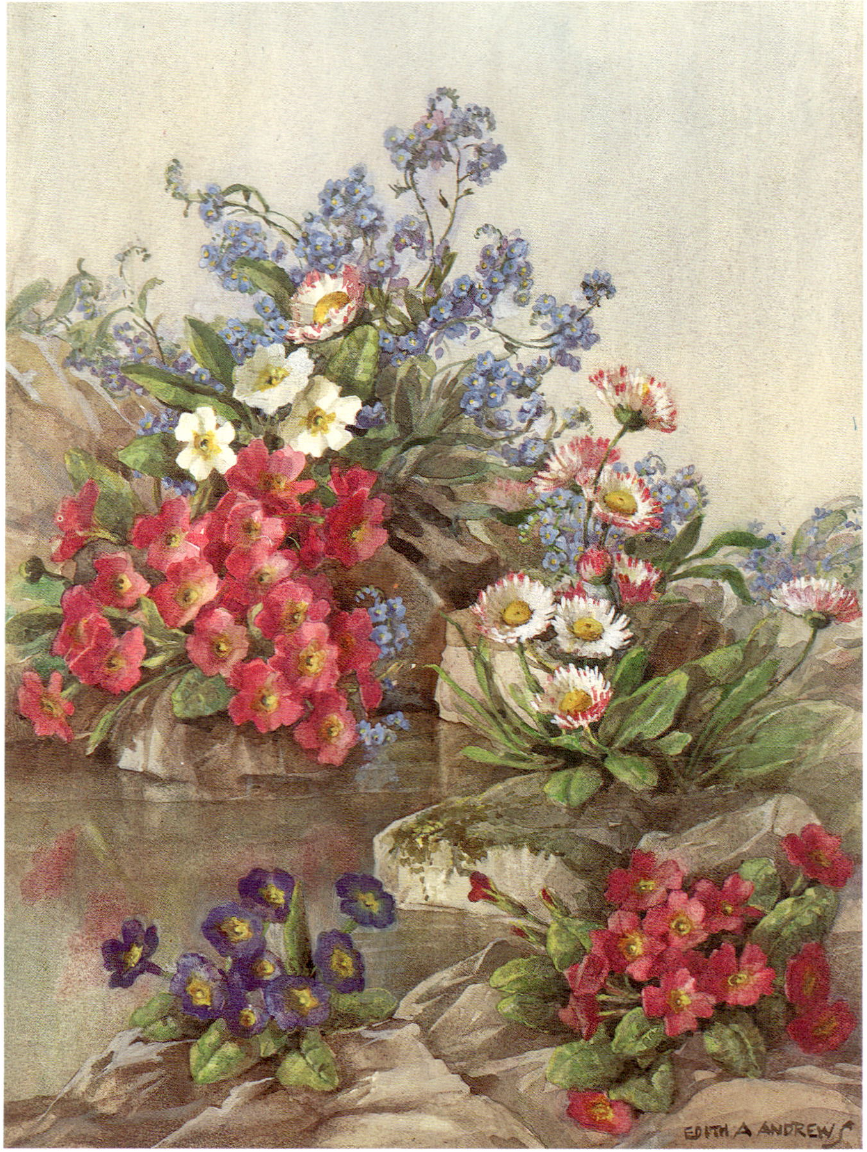

EDITH ALICE ANDREWS was a watercolour artist of flower and garden subjects and a miniaturist and illustrator. She was born Edith Alice Cubitt in 1873, the second of four children of Herbert Cundall Cubitt and his wife Alice, at St John's, South London; the Cubitts were originally a Norfolk family and an ancestor had married Joseph Stannard, an eminent member of the Norwich School of painters. She was educated by governess at home and trained at Kensington School of Art. She began exhibiting her paintings in 1900, at the Royal Academy, the Royal Institute of Painters in Watercolours and also provincial galleries; she exhibited miniatures at the Paris Salon. After her father died, in 1906, she and her widowed mother lived with her brother Percy. The family were all musical; Edith sang and all the others either sang or

Beside the Pool
by Edith A Andrews

played an instrument. In 1912 she married George Andrews, a musician, and a son was born in 1914. Later she lived at High Wycombe where her husband had obtained the post of church organist. In 1929 her husband died and, being left with little money, Mrs Andrews turned back to her painting to help support herself and her son. In addition to exhibiting at galleries, for many years Mrs Andrews showed her paintings at the Chelsea Flower Show where a number were purchased by King George V and Queen Mary. They further commissioned her to paint flower and garden pictures for reproduction on Royal Christmas cards. Following the death of her husband, Mrs Andrews moved to Combe Cottage, Pembury, Kent where she had a studio; here she lived for the remainder of her life. She died in 1958.

First of the Year
by Edith A Andrews

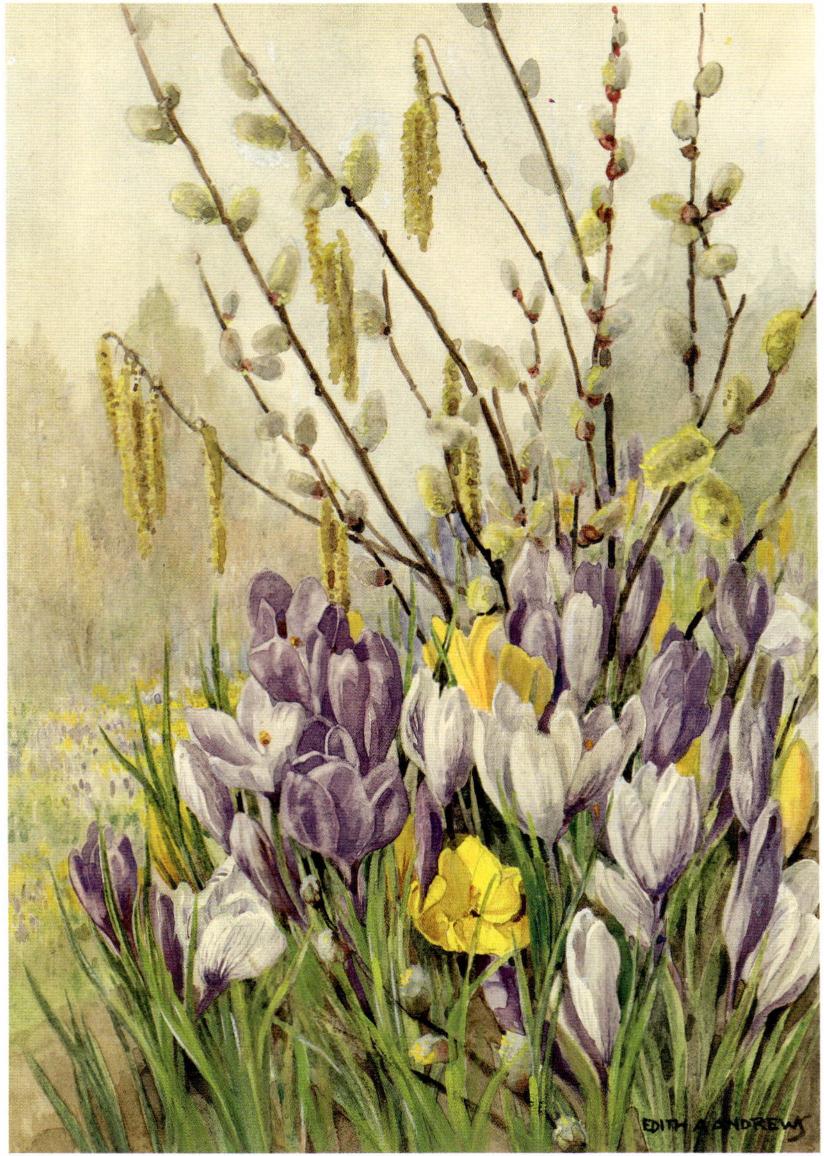

APRIL

What a lovely month, with the thought always present of the glorious displays in a few days. Think of all the wonderful Daffodils these days, the Wallflowers and Forgetmenots, filling the air with their lovely scent. The Aubretia and Alyssum on the dry walls and Erinus and Thymus between the crazy paving stones. The Tulip species, the flowering shrubs galore, especially Rhododendrons and Azaleas and don't forget to take all the old flowers off once they have finished. In the kitchen garden weeds are becoming troublesome so keep hoeing whenever possible; even if you don't see any young seedlings springing up, hoeing helps the crops. Get in your Potatoes, the first opportunity. Sow all your Winter Broccoli, Kales, Savoys and Winter Cabbage. Always think about the Winter crops, they take a long time to grow. Sow horn variety Carrots every three weeks, two or three rows, also Cabbage Lettuce, Radishes every eighteen days. Keep the Asparagus cut regularly, even the sprue is fine growth, most suitable for soups.

The Lavender Walk by William F Ashburner

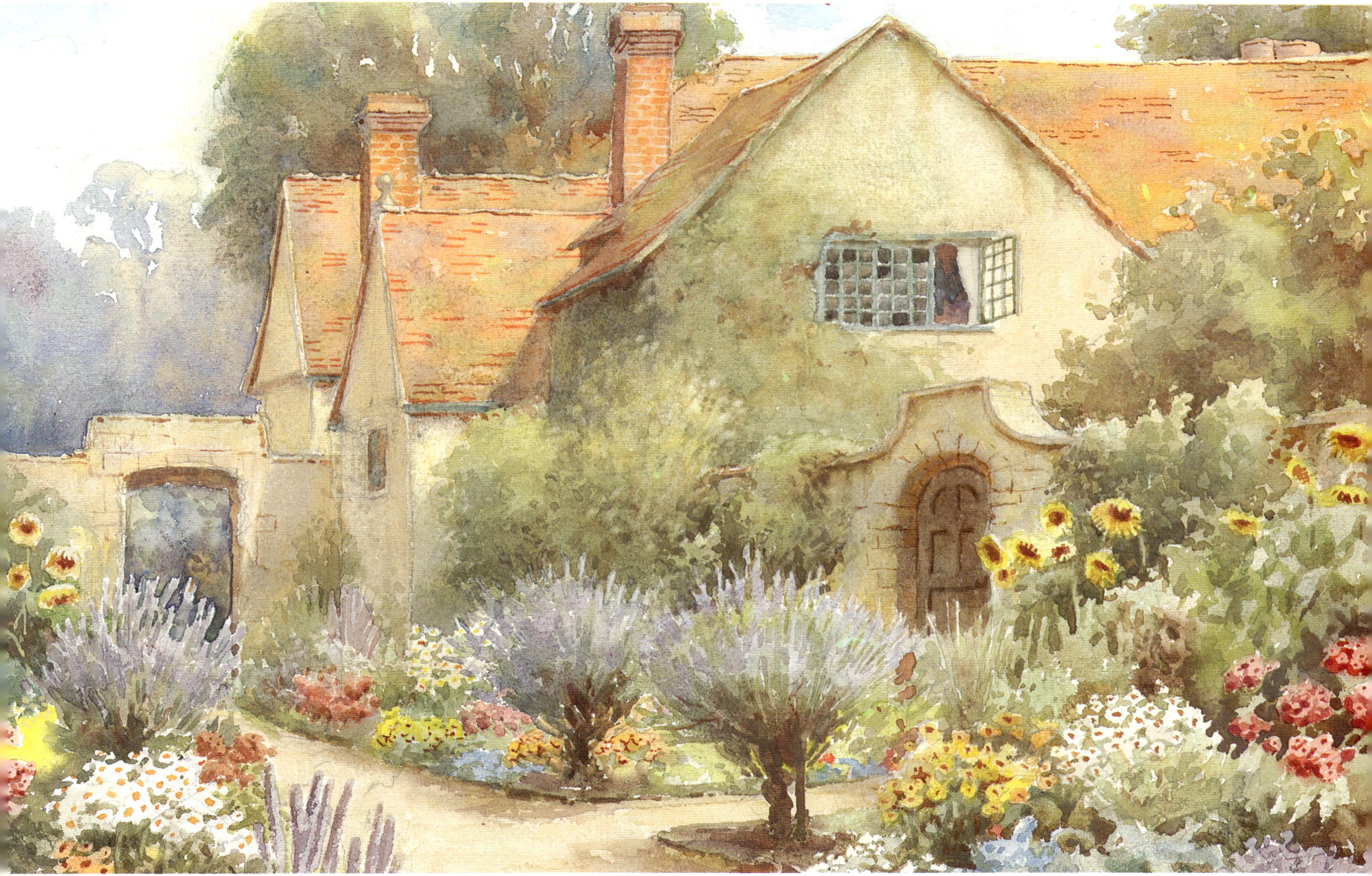

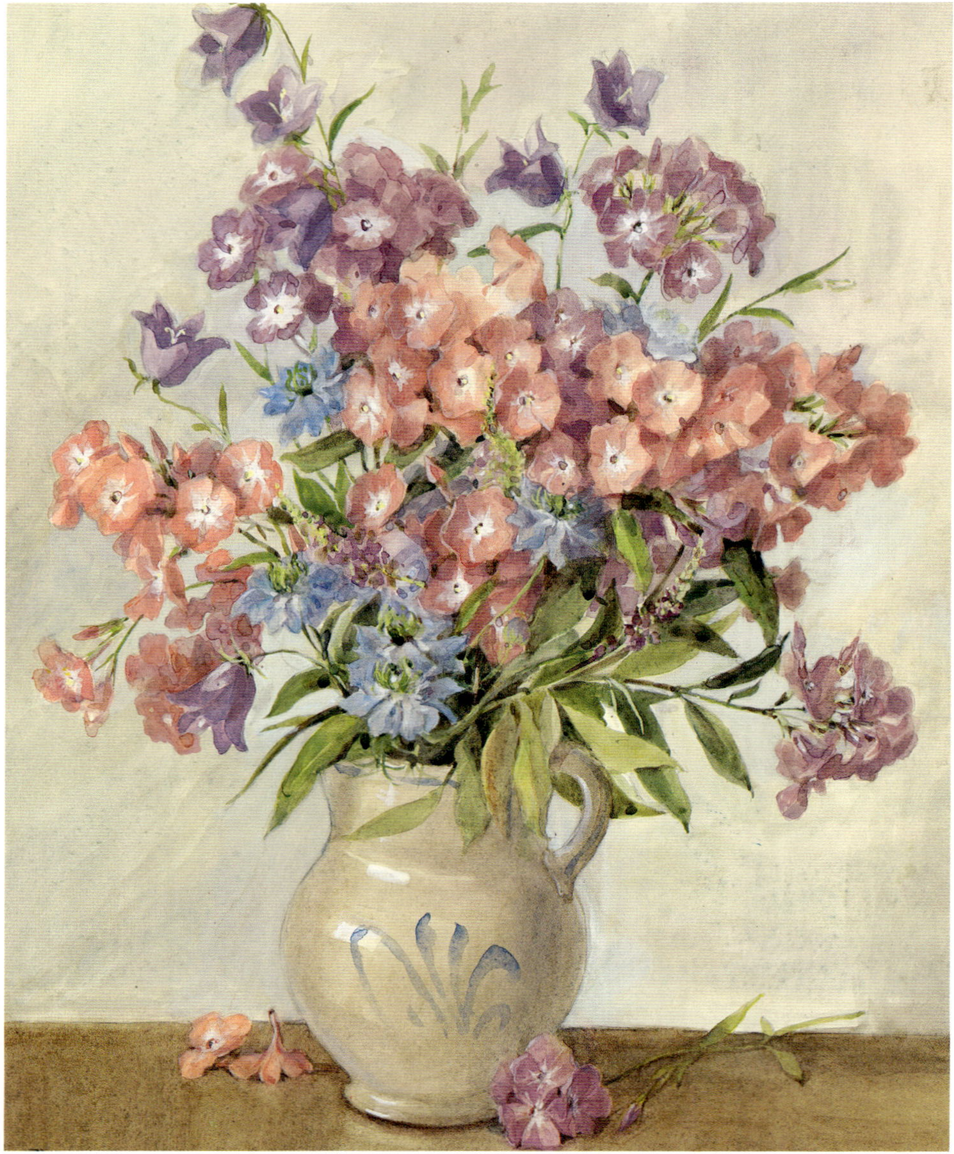

Sweet letters of the angel tongue,
  I've loved ye long and well,
And never have failed in your
    fragrance sweet
To find some secret spell, –
A charm that has bound me with
    witching power,
For mine is the old belief,
That midst your sweets and midst
    your bloom,
There's a soul in every leaf!

M M Ballou

Phlox and Love-in-a-Mist
by Edith A Andrews

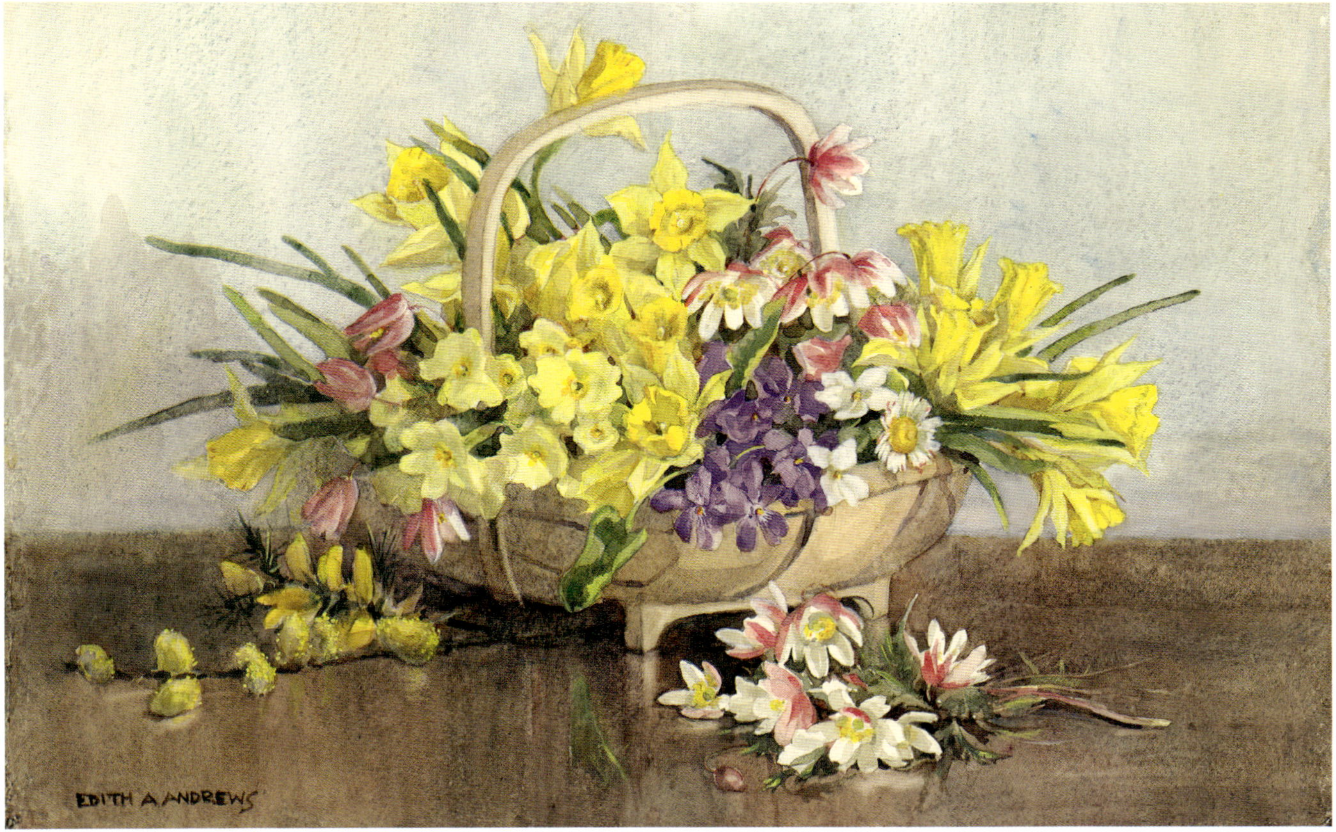

Spring Gathered by Edith A Andrews

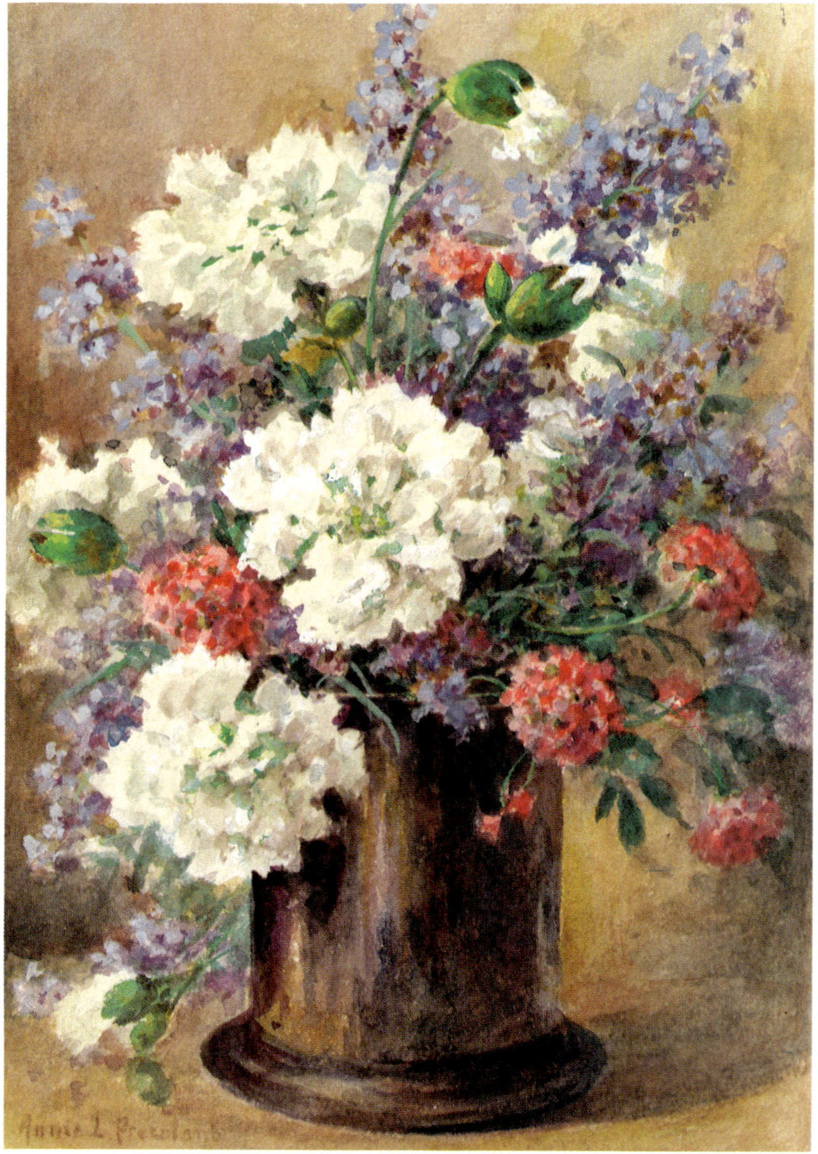

ANNIE LOUISA PRESSLAND was a watercolour painter of flowers, gardens and still life subjects in a full-bodied and distinctive style. She was born on 2nd July 1862, the daughter of Caleb Pressland and his first wife Louisa of Wandsworth, South London; she was baptised in Brighton. She trained at the Slade School of Art and exhibited between 1892 and 1923 at the Society of Women Artists, the Royal Institute of Painters in Watercolours, the London Salon and galleries in Liverpool, Birmingham and Manchester. In the 1920s, after her father's death, she moved to live with her stepmother, her father's third wife Winnie, and together they resided at 29 Gracedale Road, Streat-

White Pinks and Catmint
by Annie L Pressland

ham; this somewhat demanding relationship restricted Miss Pressland's work and exhibiting opportunities for a number of years. She was only able fully to resume her artistic career after the death of her stepmother, when she moved to Oakleigh, Felbridge, Sussex in 1927 to enjoy her painting and artistic life. Much of her time was occupied in travelling around the country painting private gardens and in 1928 she was commissioned by Frances, Countess of Warwick, to produce a series of ten paintings of Easton Lodge, Suffolk. She was a tall, somewhat autocratic figure with a penchant for straw hats embroidered with raffia flowers. She died in 1933 aged 71 years.

Freesia and Parma Violets
by Annie L Pressland

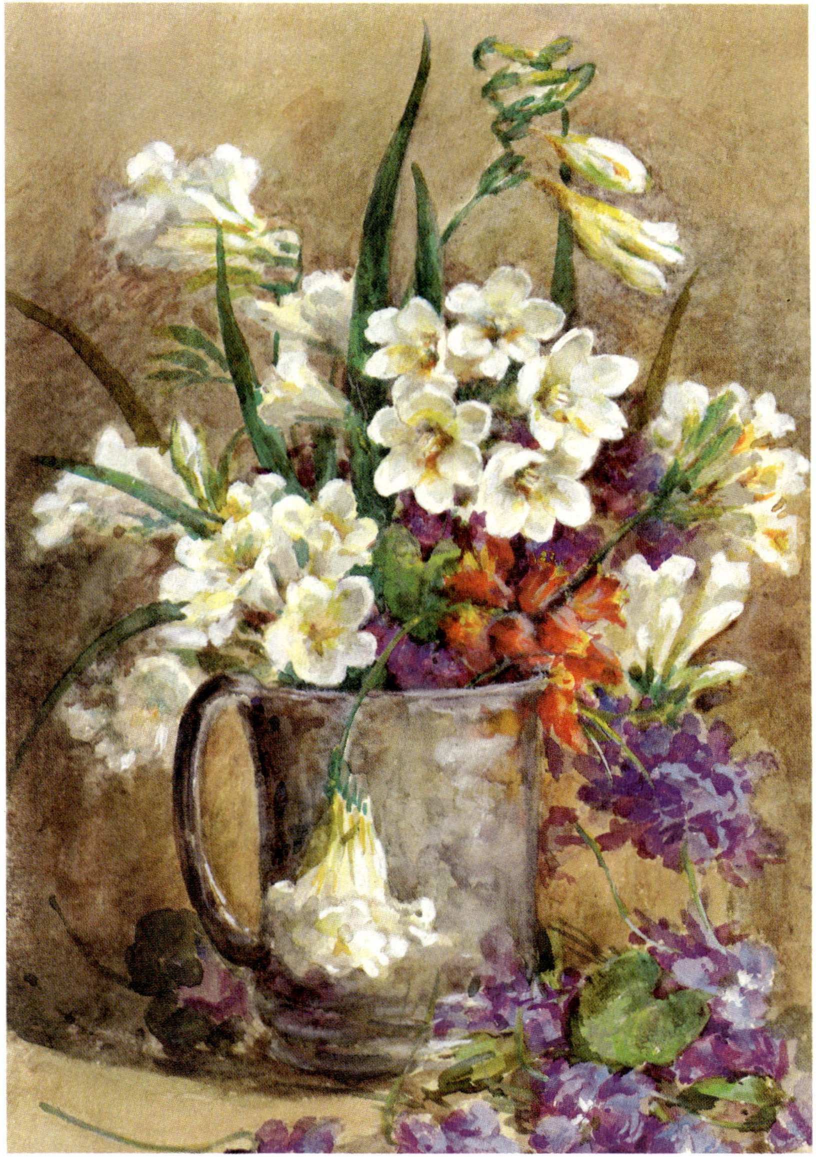

MAY

Is it possible to imagine anything more lovely than a garden full of flowers during the month of May. Pride of place must go to the Tulips however and the Bluebells in the woods, with Lily of the Valley, together with all the tints of the new-born foliage on the trees and shrubs; the long yellow chains of Laburnum, the Lilac. What a delicate scent those trusses have! The fruit blossom on the Apple, Pear and Cherry trees, and the Strawberries growing fast and showing their beautiful flowers, as attractive as the fruit I always think; only, have protection at hand in case of a late frost. The kitchen garden filled with the young seedlings and a promise of things near at hand. The Potatoes thriving and earthed up, the Celery trench out, Runner and Dwarf Beans sown and don't forget a row of the Yellow Waxpods – they're superb; outdoor Tomatoes put out the last week. Oh it's a gorgeous month.

Wistaria Cottage by Howard Walford

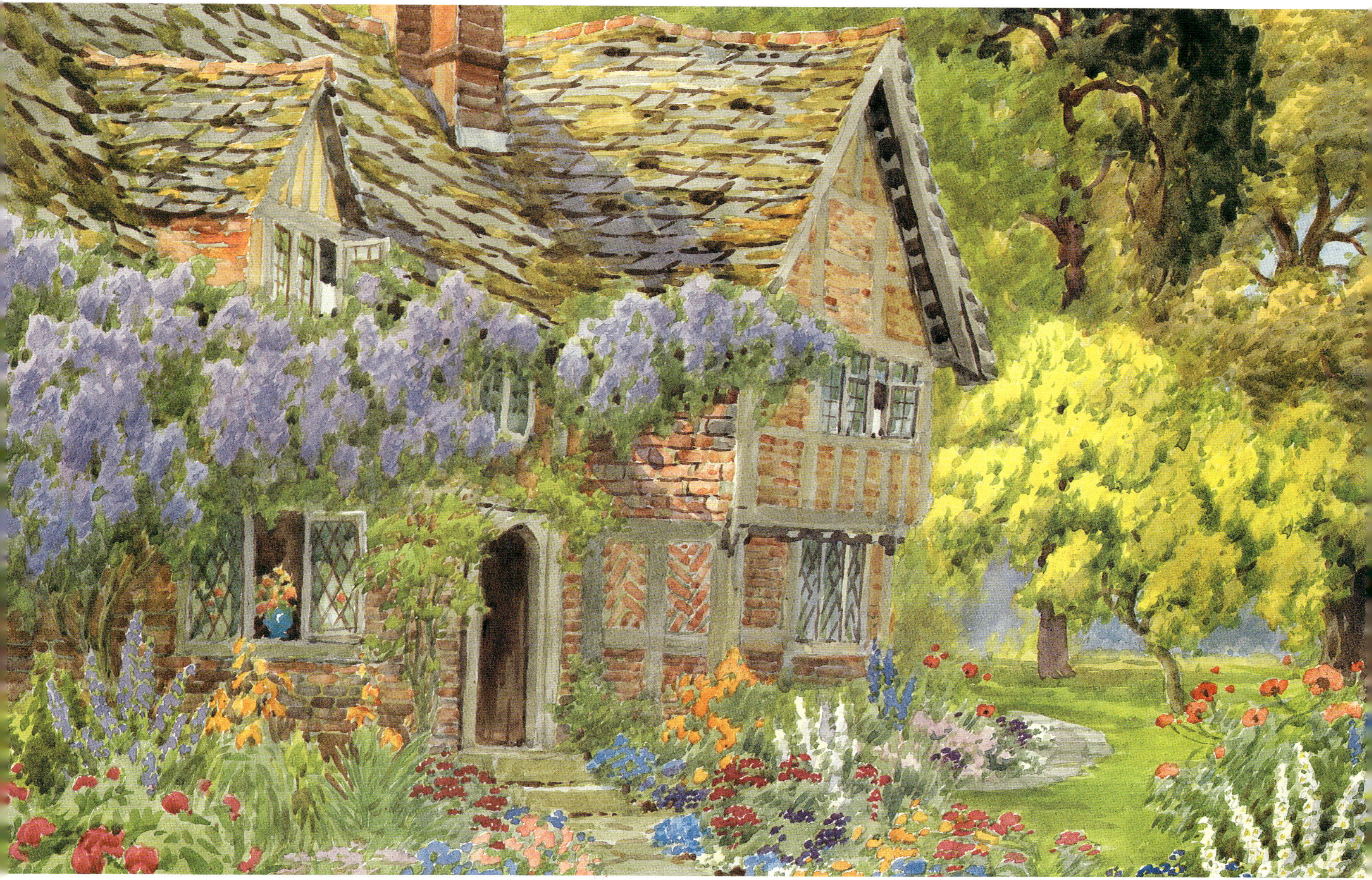

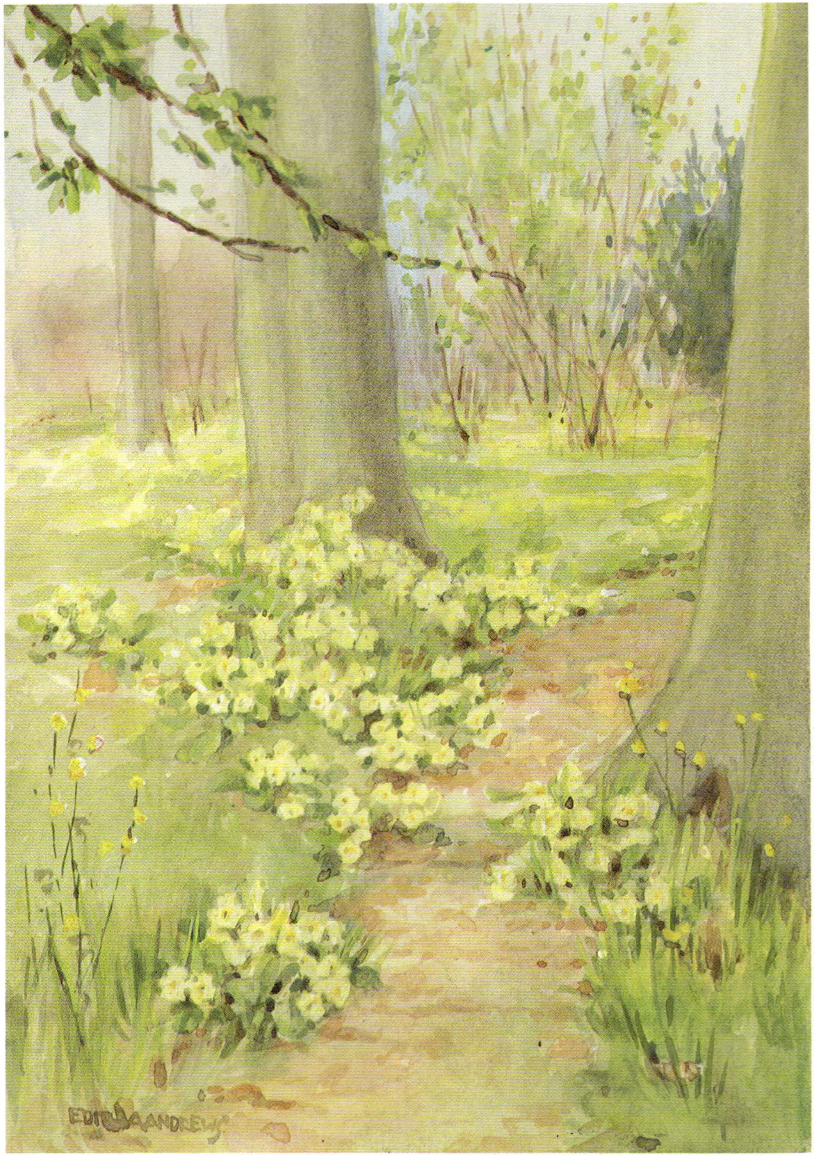

Welcome, pale primrose! starting up
between
Dead matted leaves of ash and oak
that strew
The every lawn, the wood, and
spinney through.
'Mid creeping moss and ivy's darker
green;
How much thy presence beautifies
the ground!
How sweet thy modest unaffected
pride
Glows on the sunny bank and
wood's warm side

John Clare

The Primrose Path
by Edith A Andrews

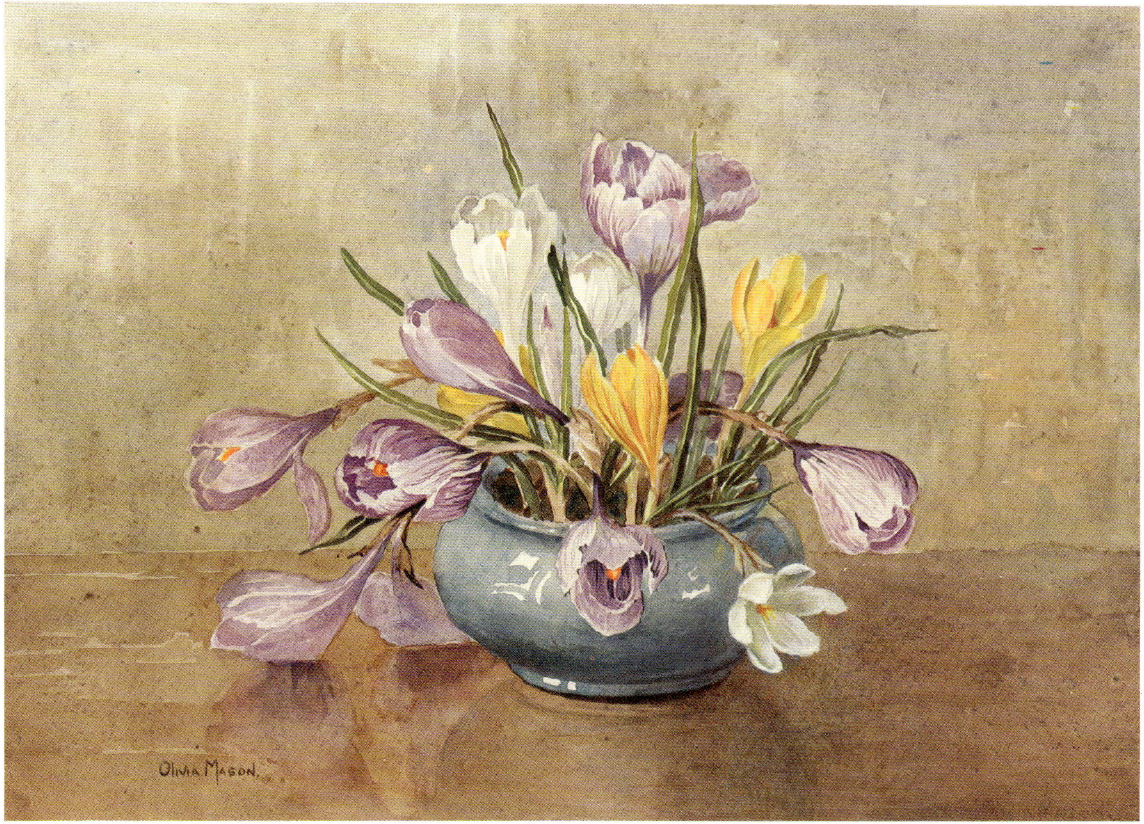

Crocuses by Olivia Mason

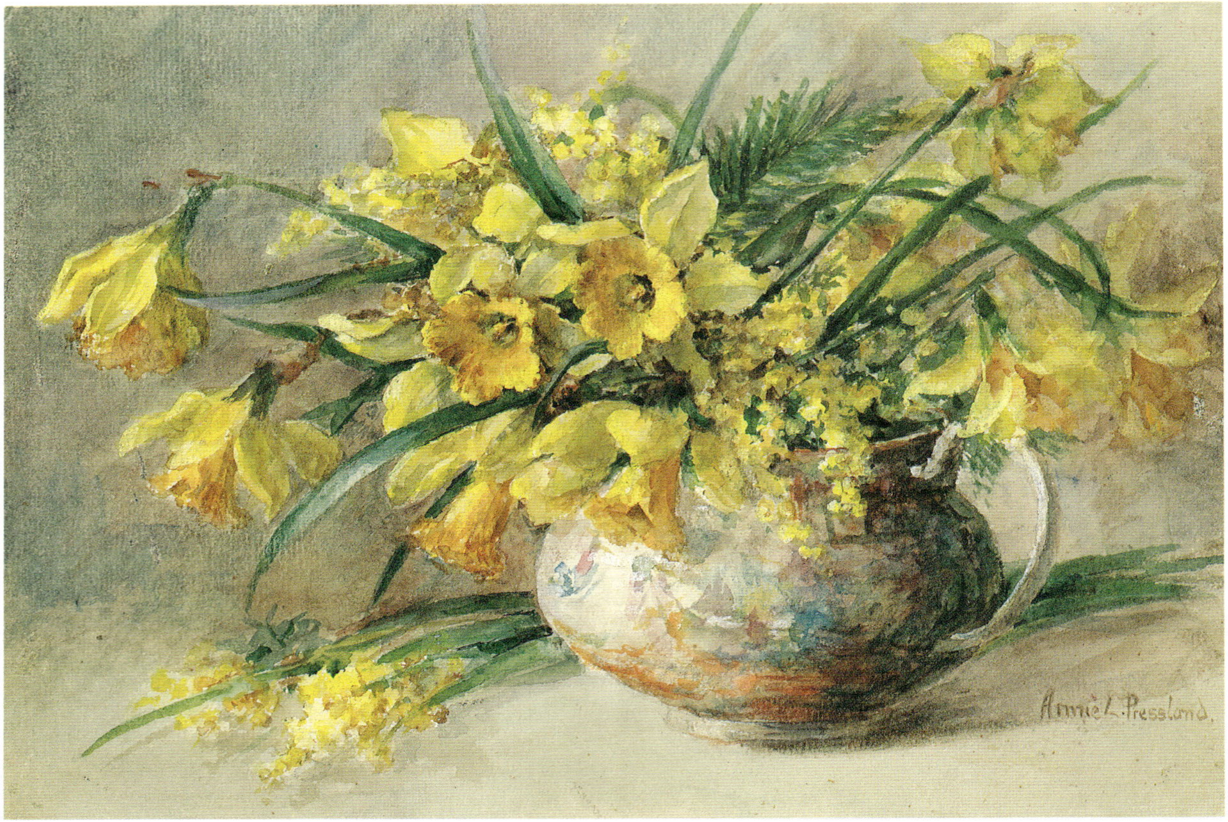

Daffodils and Mimosa by Annie L Pressland

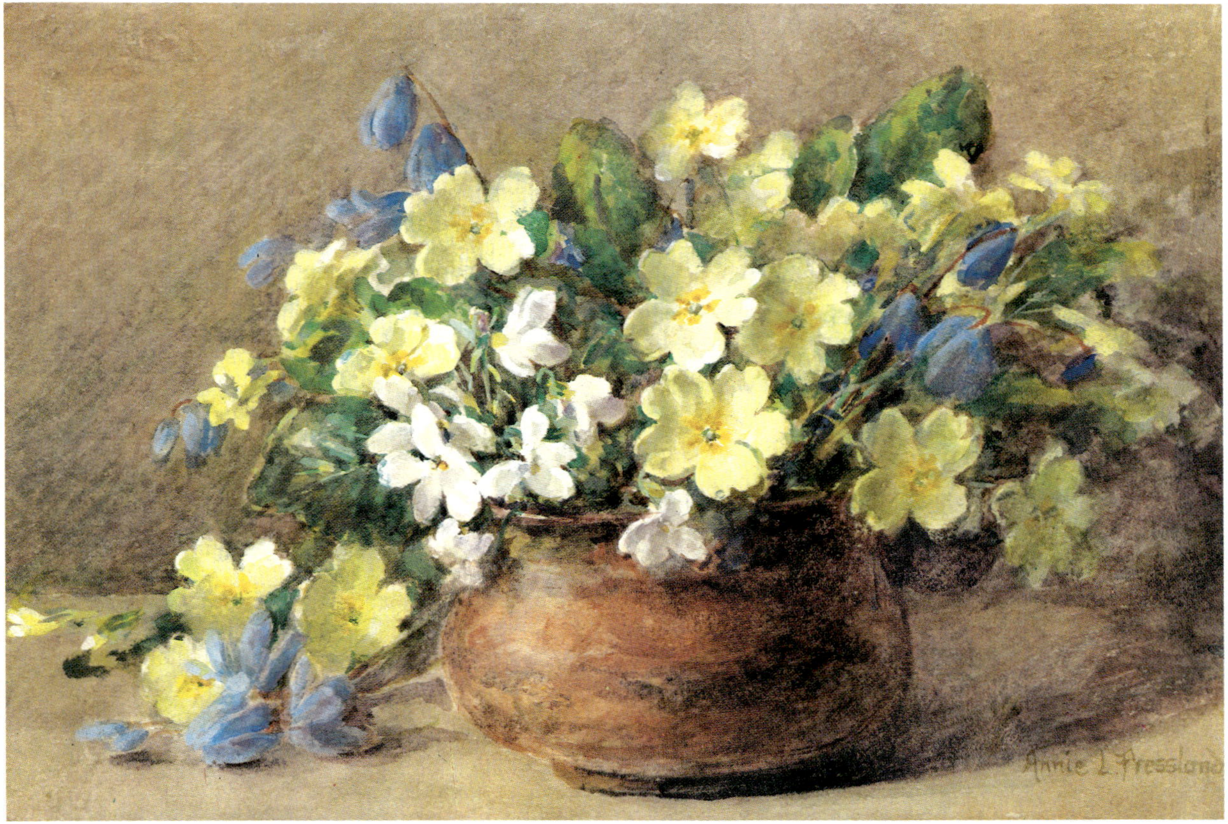

Primroses, Violets and Scylla by Annie L Pressland

JUNE

After a very busy Spring, June begins to repay you in many ways. The first Beans and Peas, new Potatoes, young Carrots and Lettuce. The sun's really warm. Finish cutting the Asparagus about the middle of the month, dress the bed with agricultural salt and let all the growth grow, but keep down the weeds. Plant out your Celery, Tomatoes and tender things raised under cover. Sow late Peas, another row of Runner Beans, Sweetcorn and small Bush Marrows, together with the successional crops of Carrots, Beet and Lettuces. Place some straw under the Strawberries and place the nets over early in the month. Start thinning your Gooseberries for tarts. Plant out your tender Summer flowering plants, Geraniums, Begonias, Stocks, Asters, Tobaccos, Petunias, Marigolds, and all the well known plants. The Roses make up the display during the period of removing the Spring flowers and the planting of Summer things. If you love blue don't forget the Ipomea. Watch the Roses closely to see no suckers escape and remove all dead flowers; don't let any seed pods form. If you do this the Roses will never fail to give you blooms and pleasure.

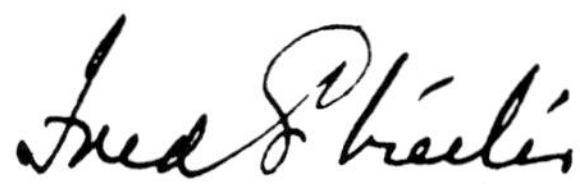

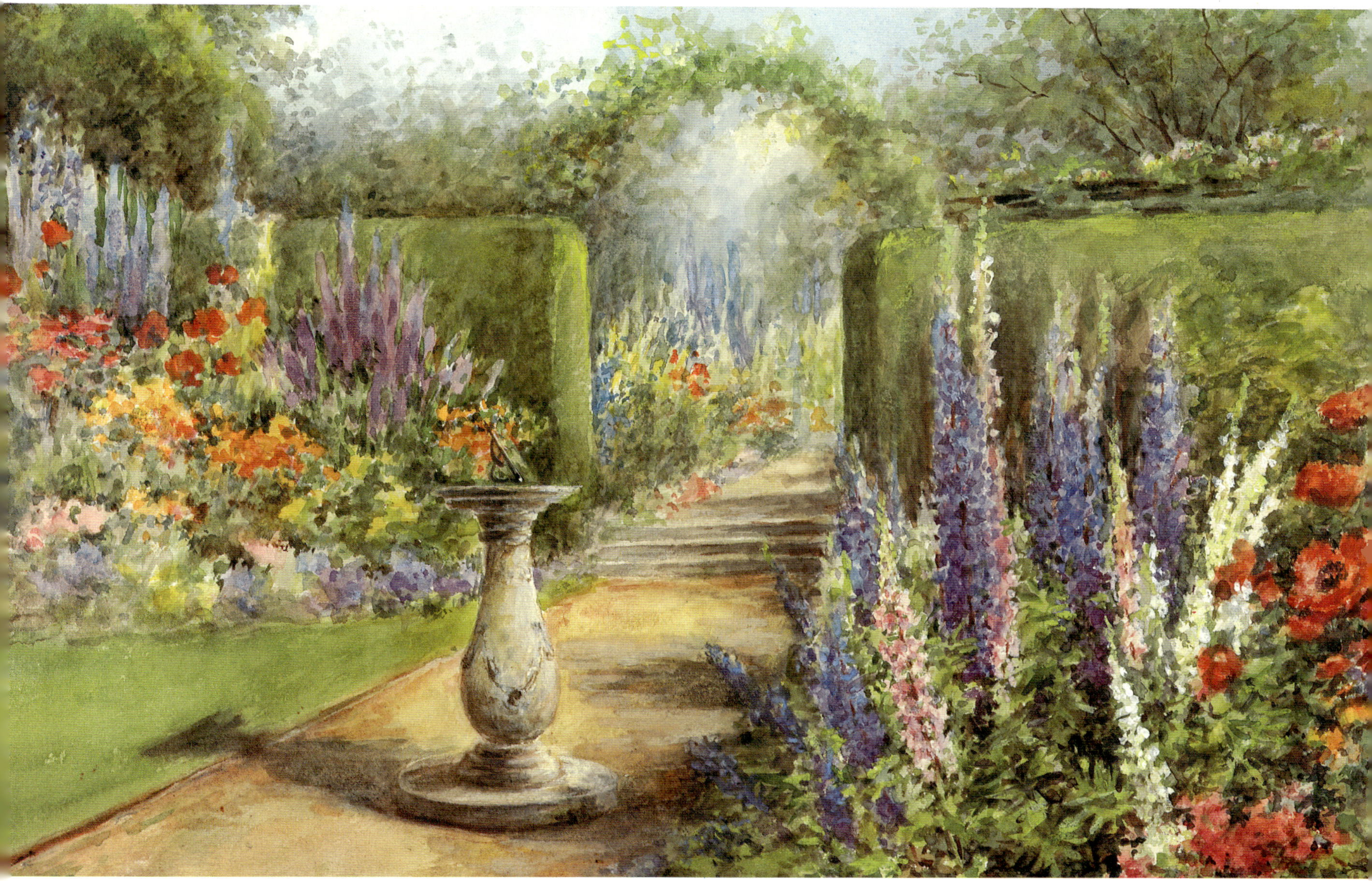

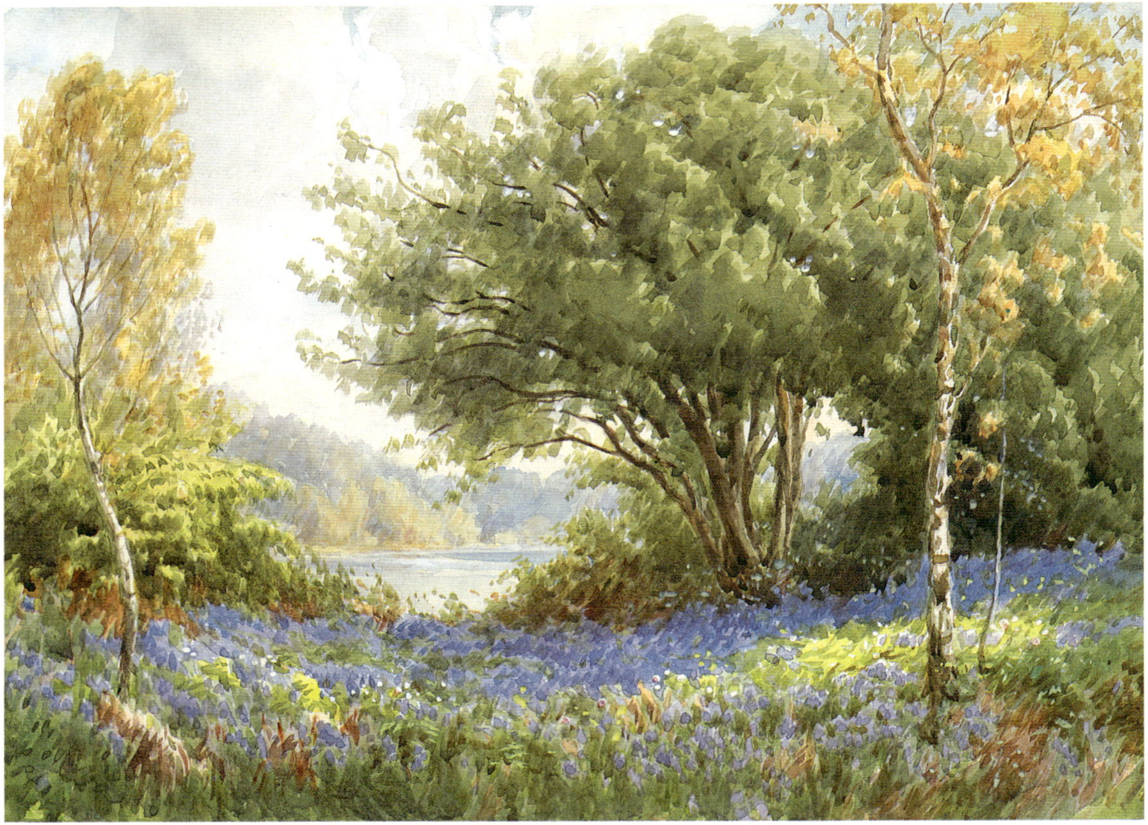

Bluebells by Howard Walford

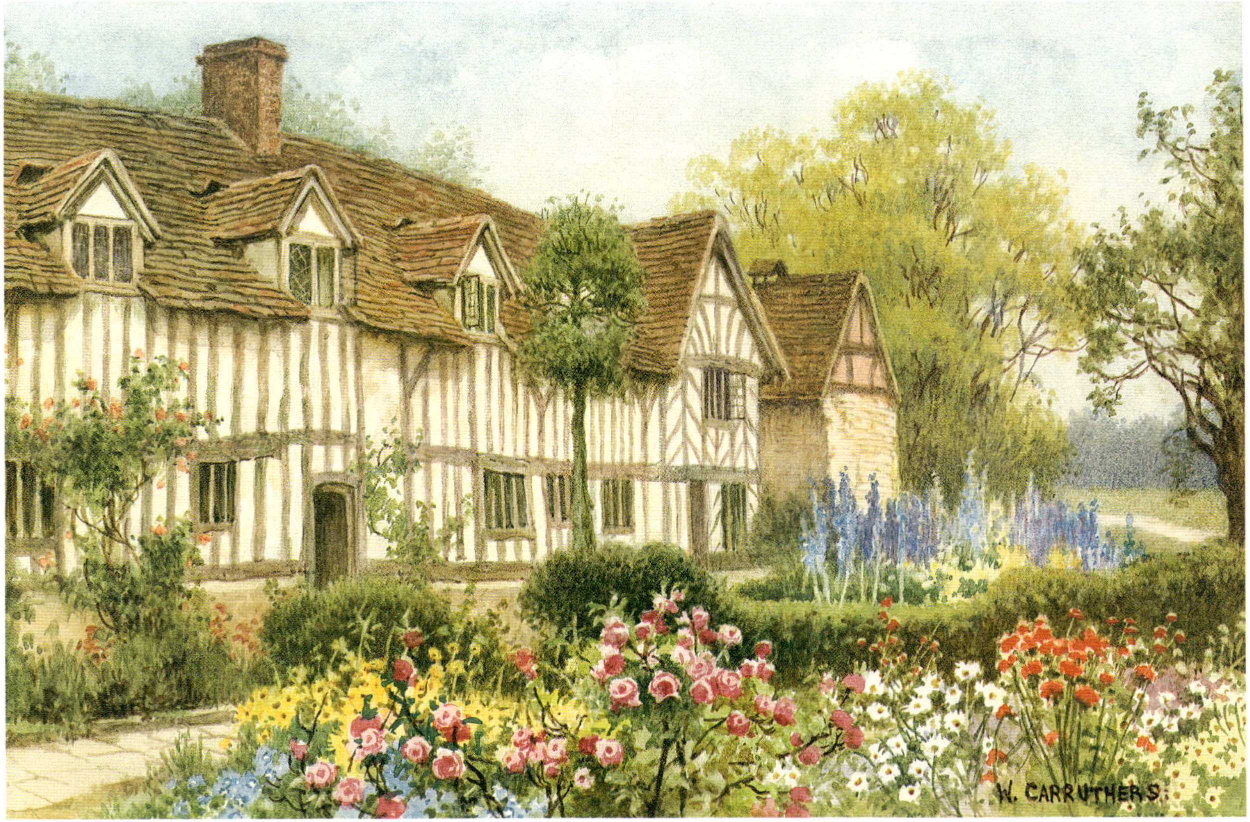

Mary Arden's House, Wilmcote by W Carruthers Affleck

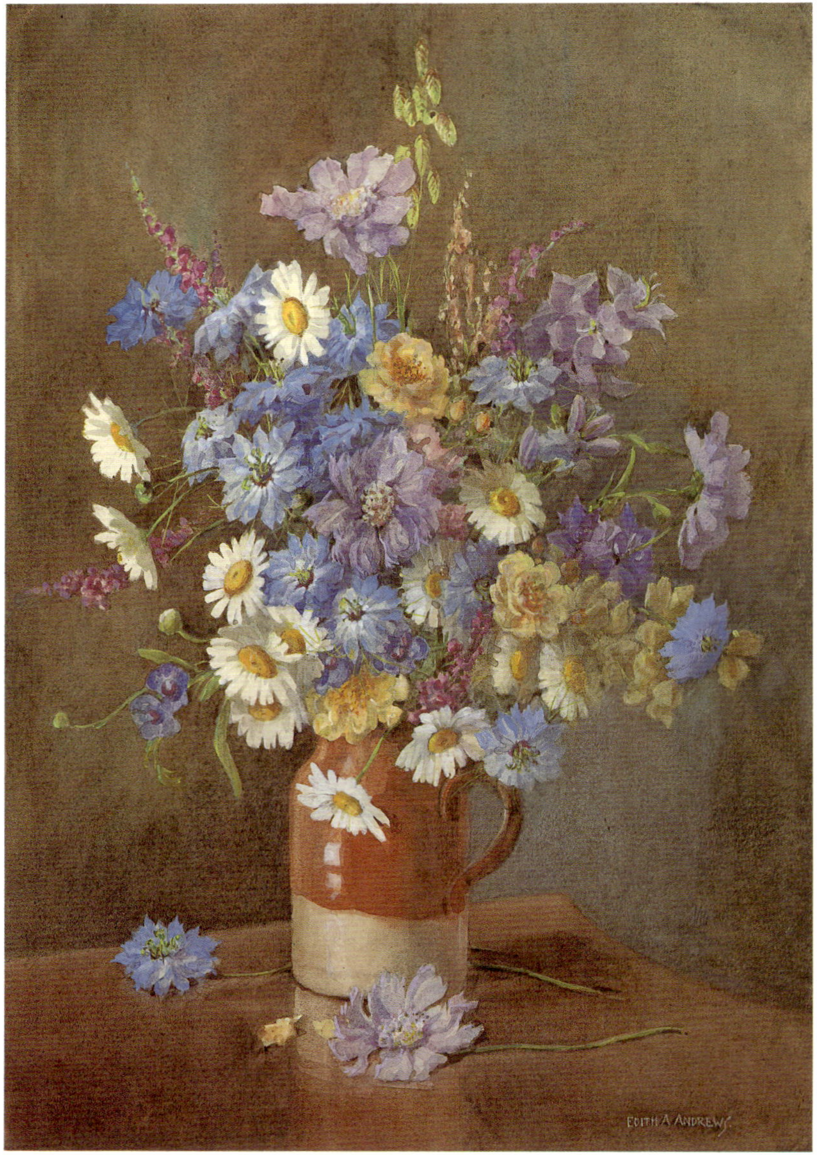

WILLIAM AFFLECK was a painter of landscapes, cottages, flowers, gardens, genre and rustic scenes in oil and watercolour. He was born at Rochdale, Lancashire in 1869 and trained at Heatherley's, South Kensington and Lambeth Schools of Art. He exhibited at London galleries from 1890, at the Royal Academy, frequently, from 1891, at the Royal Institute of Painters in Watercolour and the Royal Society of British Artists; he was a member of the London Sketch Club. He also painted for J Salmon Ltd, Art Printers and Publishers of Sevenoaks, Kent for reproduction purposes and these works he signed either William Carruthers or W.C., using his wife's maiden name as a pseudonym. He lived all his married life at 23 Leppoc Road, Clapham, South London where he died in 1949.

From a Cottage Garden
by Edith A Andrews

Flowers are Love's truest language;
they betray,
Like the divining rods of Magi old,
Where precious wealth lies buried,
not of gold,
But love – strong love, that never
can decay!

Park Benjamin

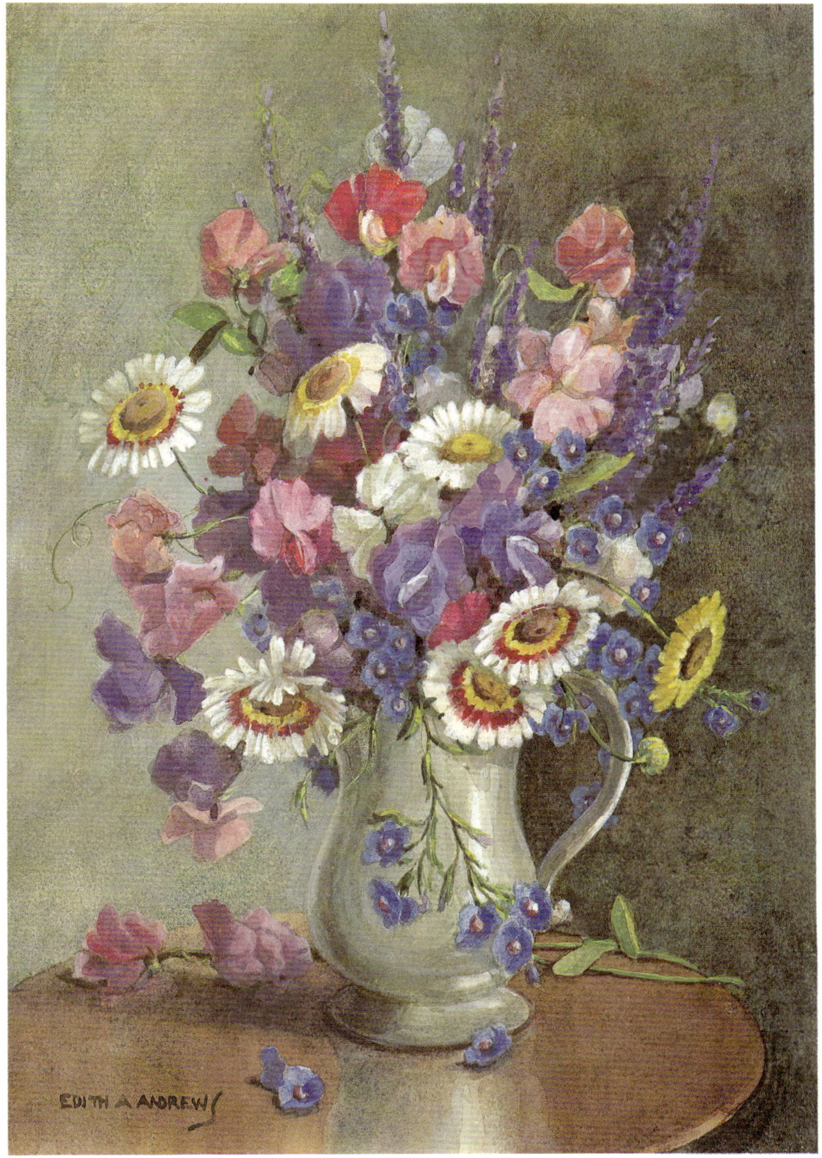

From a Mixed Border
by Edith A Andrews

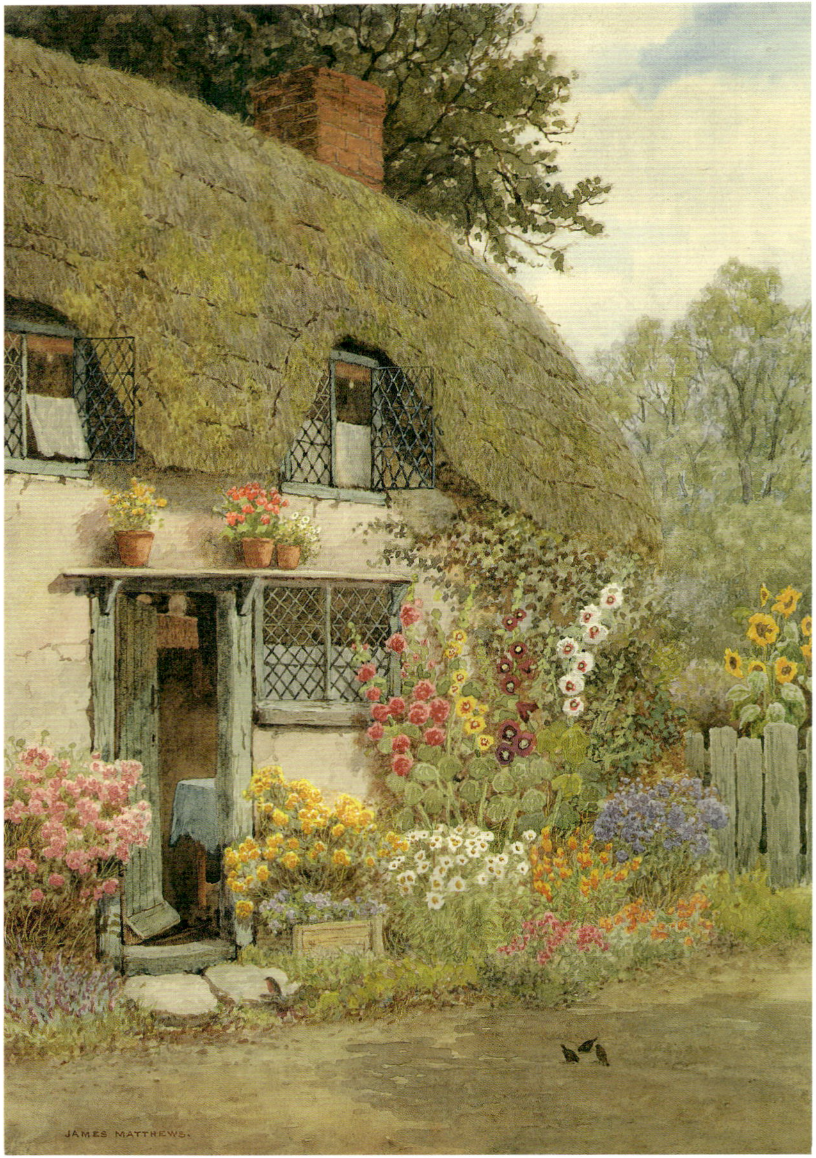

JAMES MATTHEWS was a Sussex painter of sunny, flower-filled gardens, cottages and rural scenes. He lived at Three Gables, Rudgwick near Horsham, Sussex and flourished in the later years of the 19th and the early years of the 20th centuries. His style was similar to the better-known Helen Allingham, with whom he was a nearly exact contemporary, but he was possibly less accomplished, having a tendency towards tightness of detail and a more limited freedom of expression. He died in 1929.

"Be it ever so humble . . ."
by James Matthews

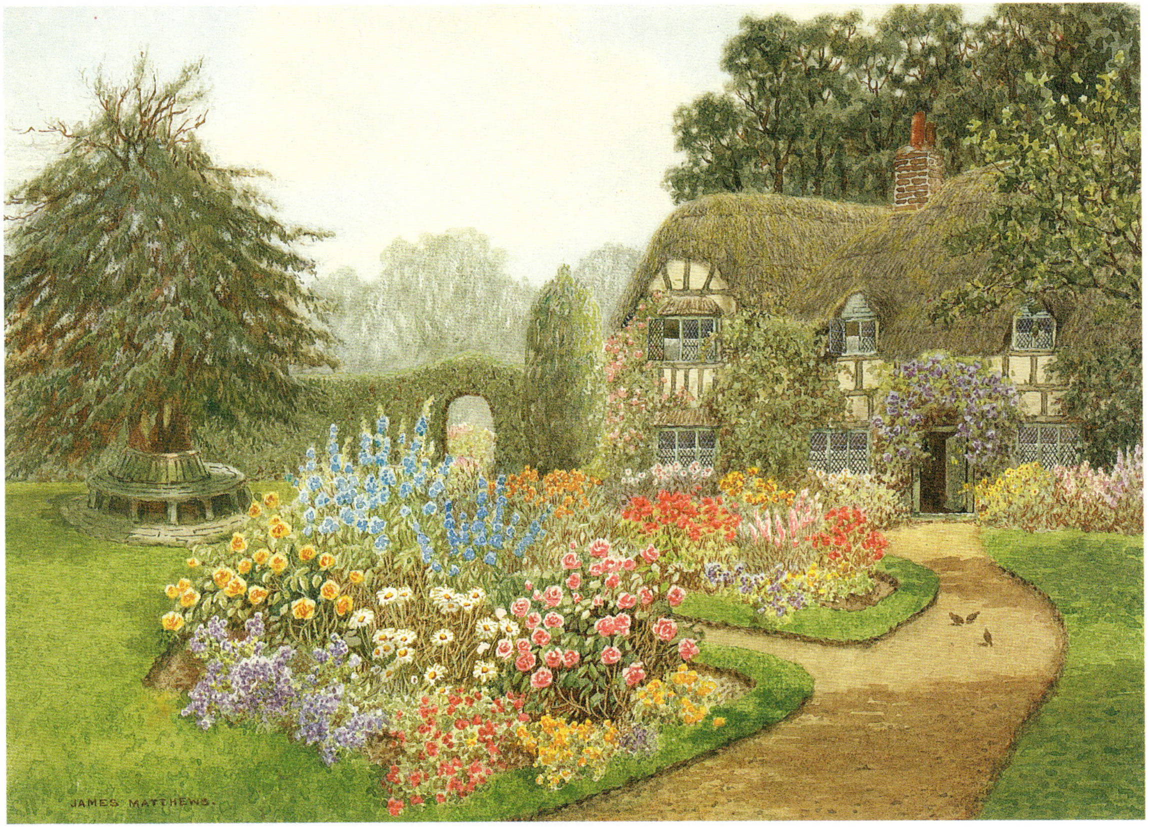

The Rectory Garden by James Matthews

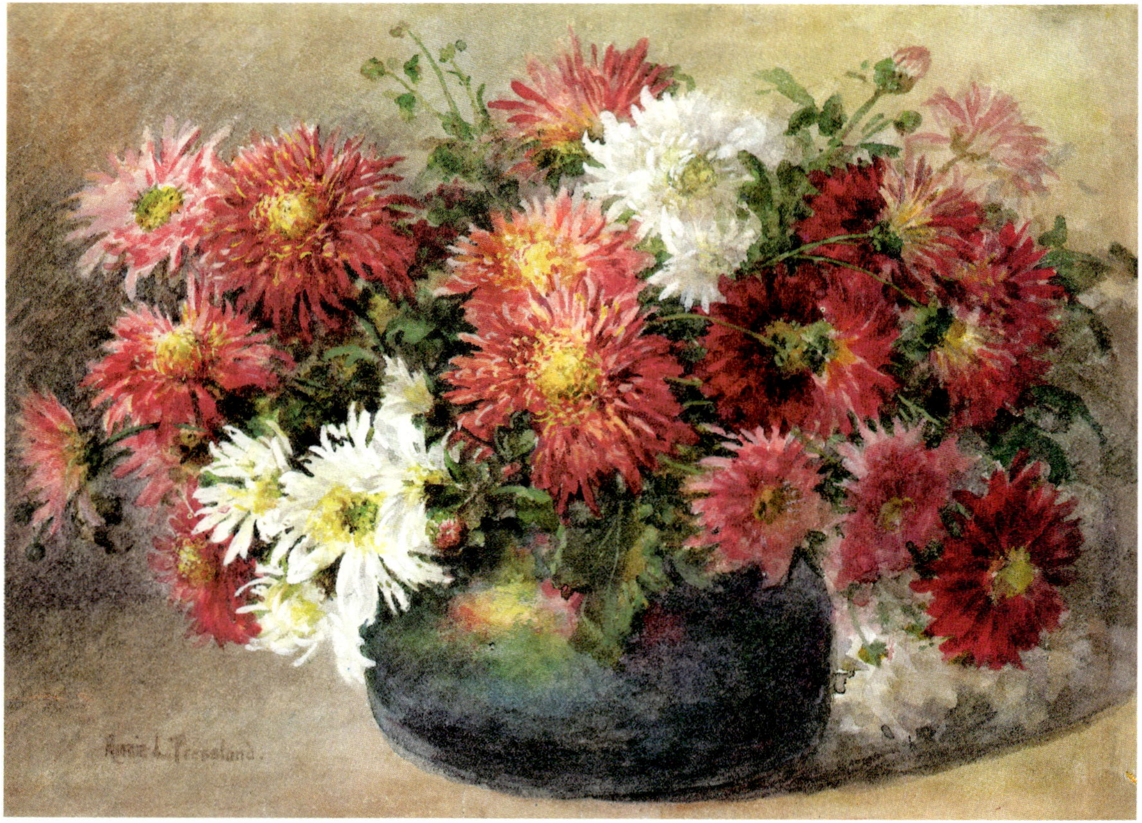

Chrysanthemums by Annie L Pressland

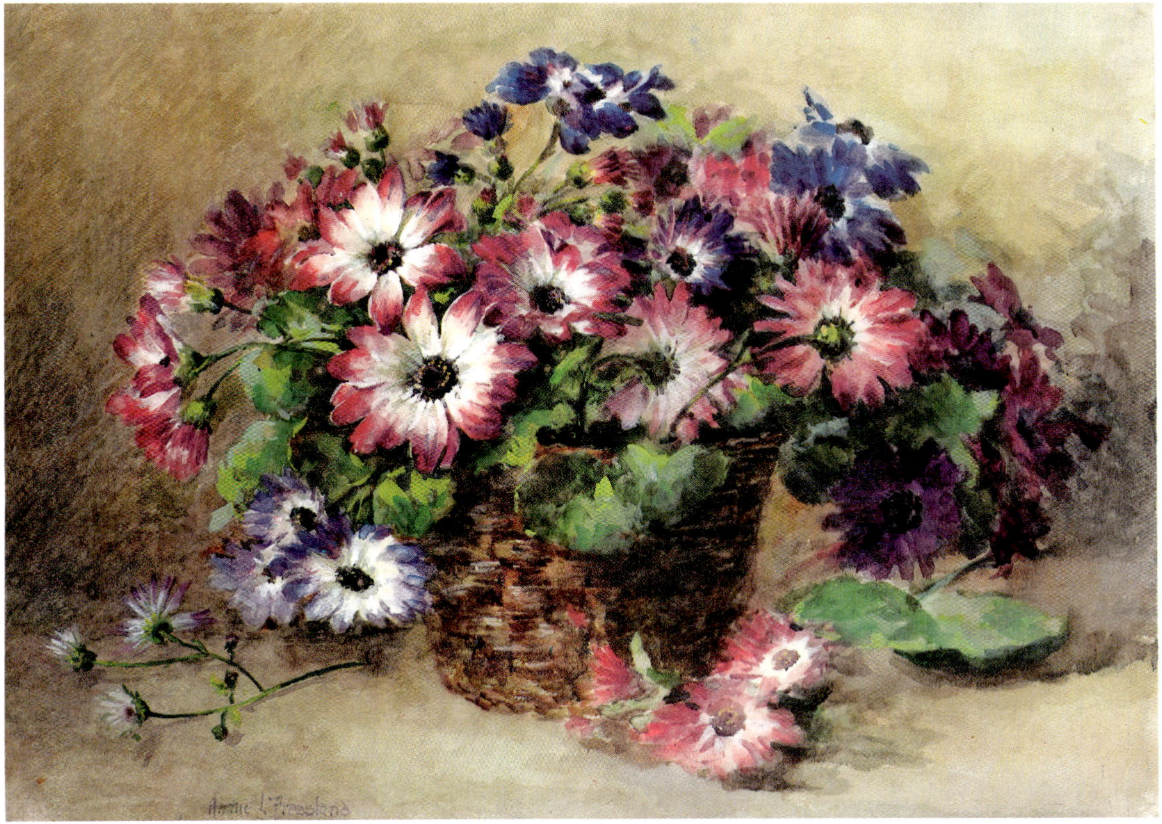

Cinerarias by Annie L Pressland

Oh, Adam was a gardener, and
God who made him sees
That half a proper gardener's work
is done upon his knees,
So when your work is finished,
you can wash your hands and pray,
For the Glory of the Garden,
that it may not pass away.
And the Glory of the Garden
it shall never pass away!

Rudyard Kipling

In an Old-World Garden by Theresa S Stannard

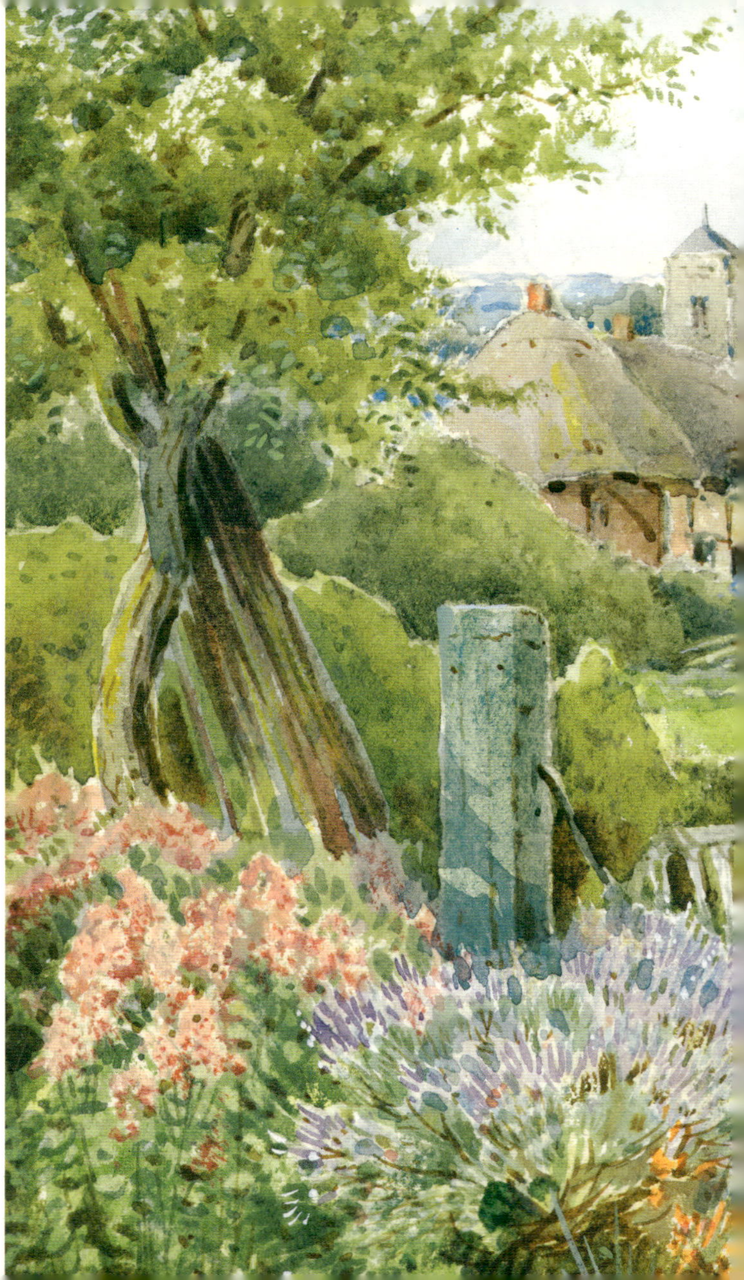

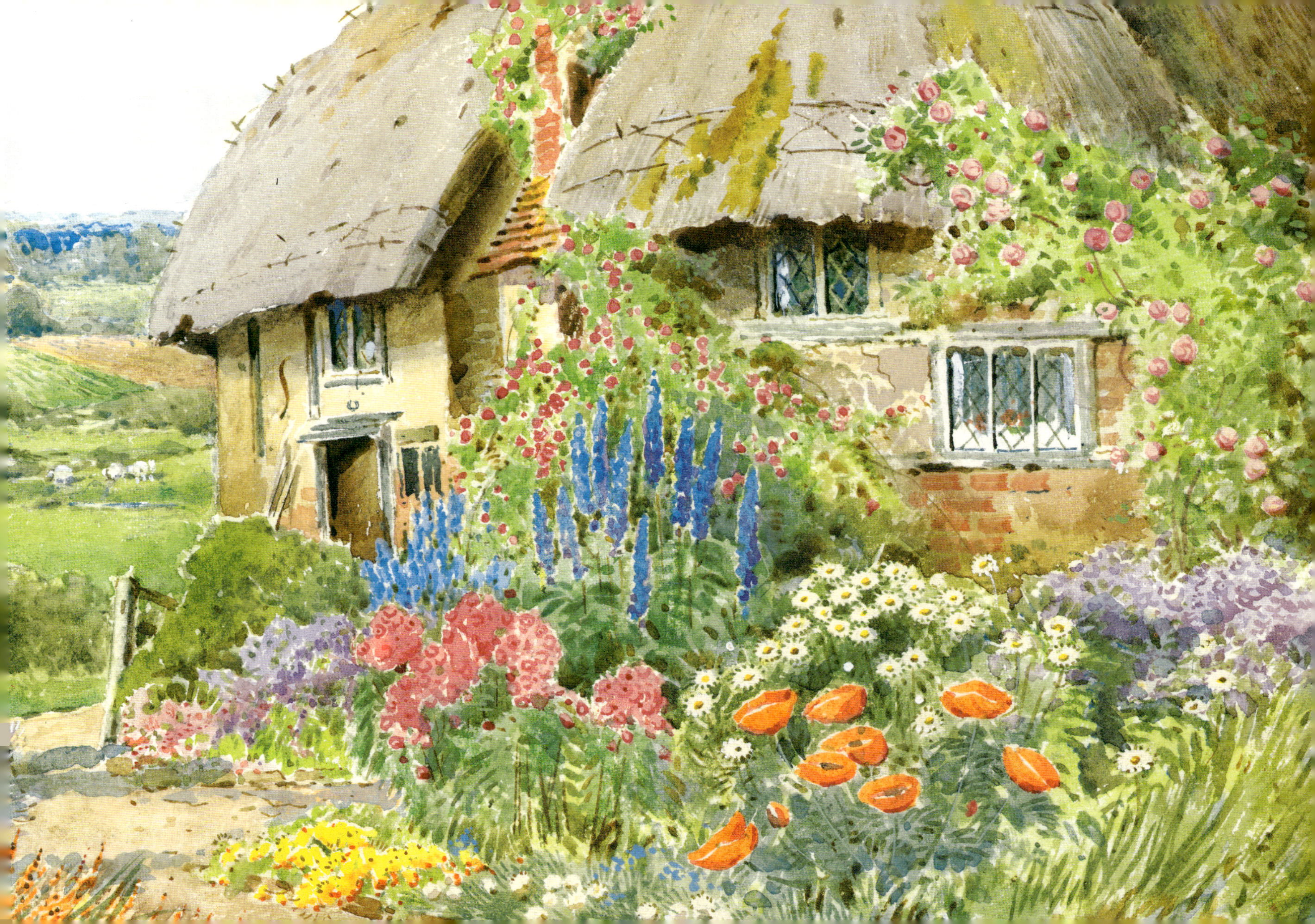

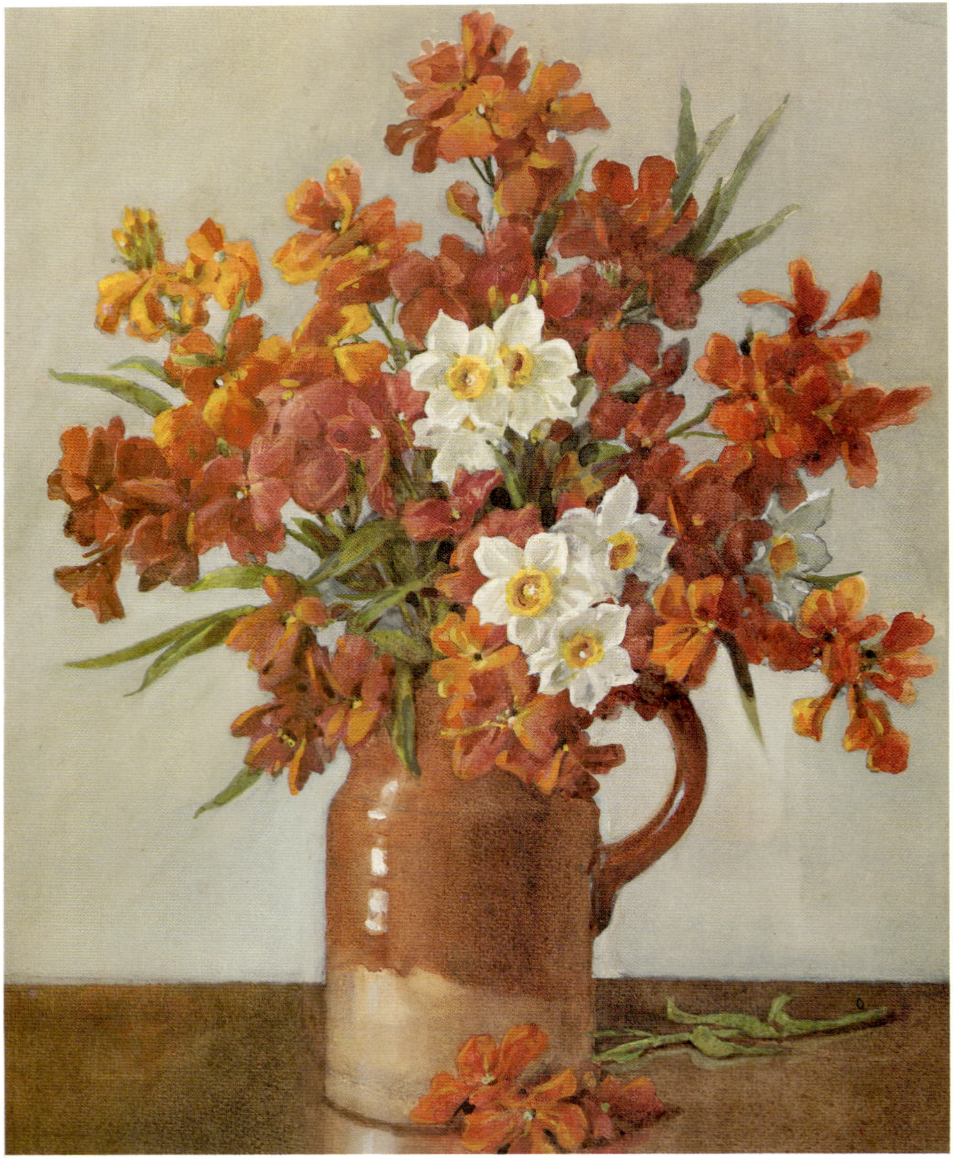

The Wall-flower – the Wall-flower,
How beautiful it blooms!
It gleams above the ruined tower,
Like sunlight over tombs;
It sheds a halo of repose
Around the wrecks of time.
To beauty give the flaunting rose,
The Wall-flower is sublime.

D M Moir

Wallflowers by Edith A Andrews

What skilful limner e'er would
choose
To paint the rainbow's varying hues,
Unless to mortal it were given
To dip his brush in dyes of heaven?
Sir Walter Scott

Summer Flowers
by Dorcie Sykes

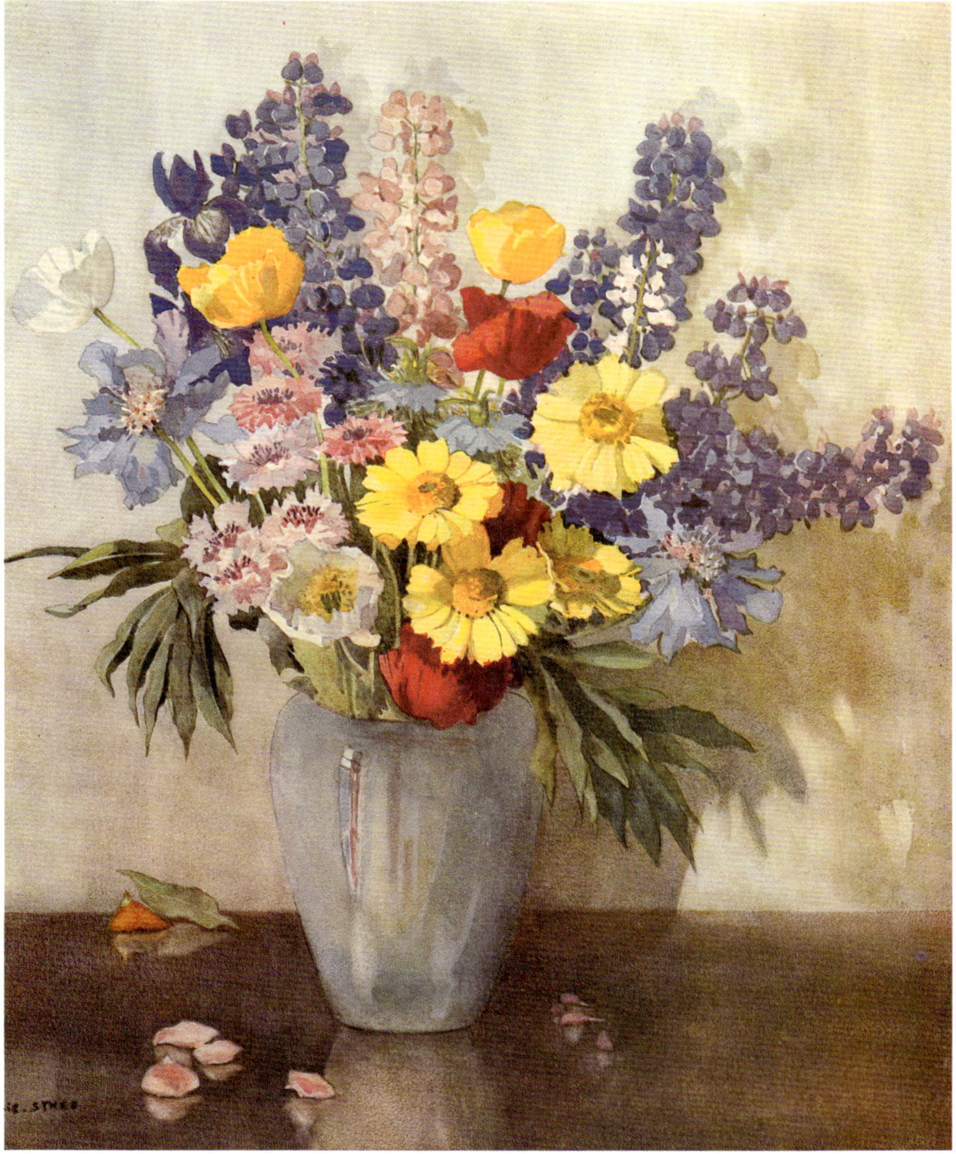

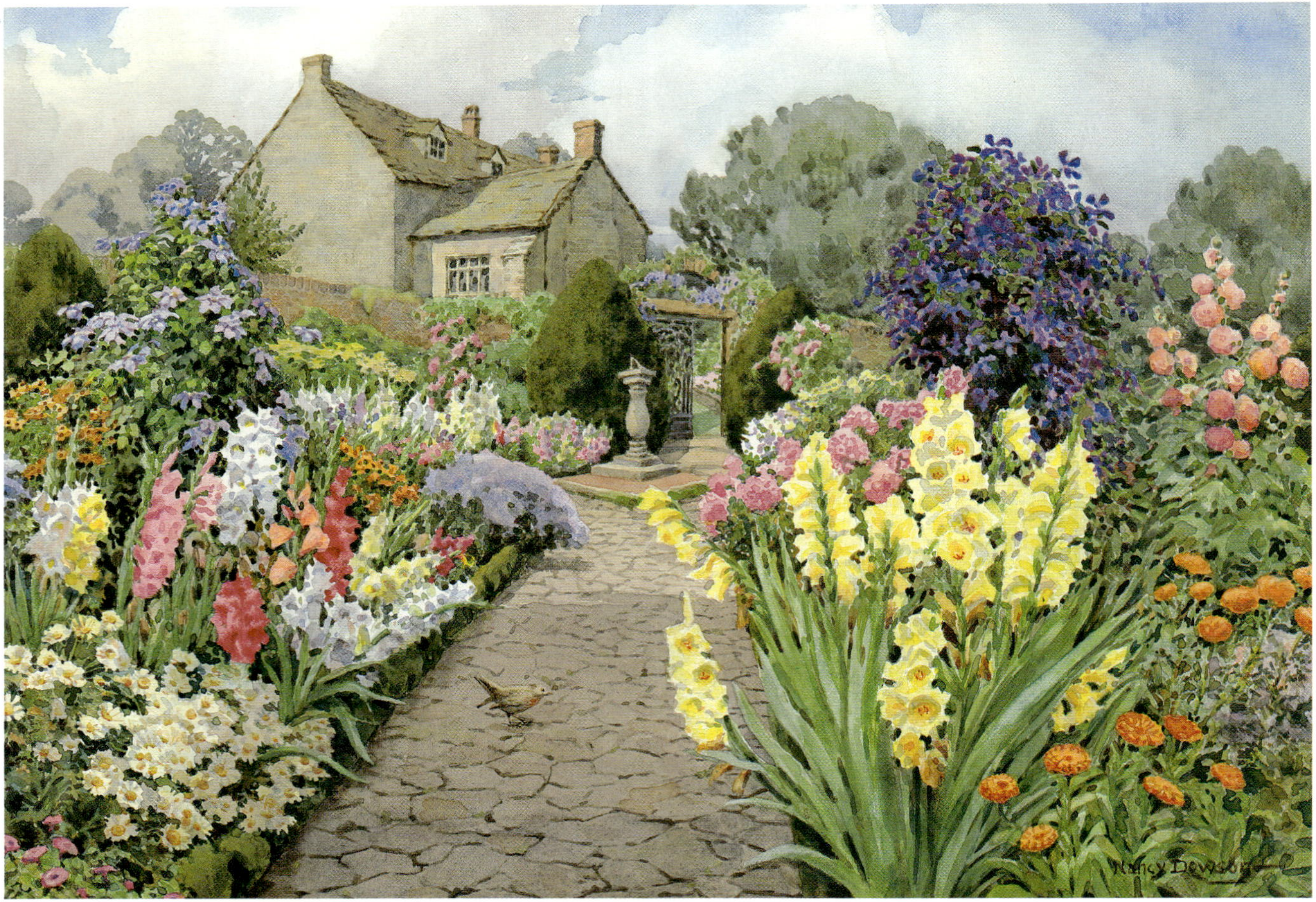

The Sundial Walk by Nancy Dowson

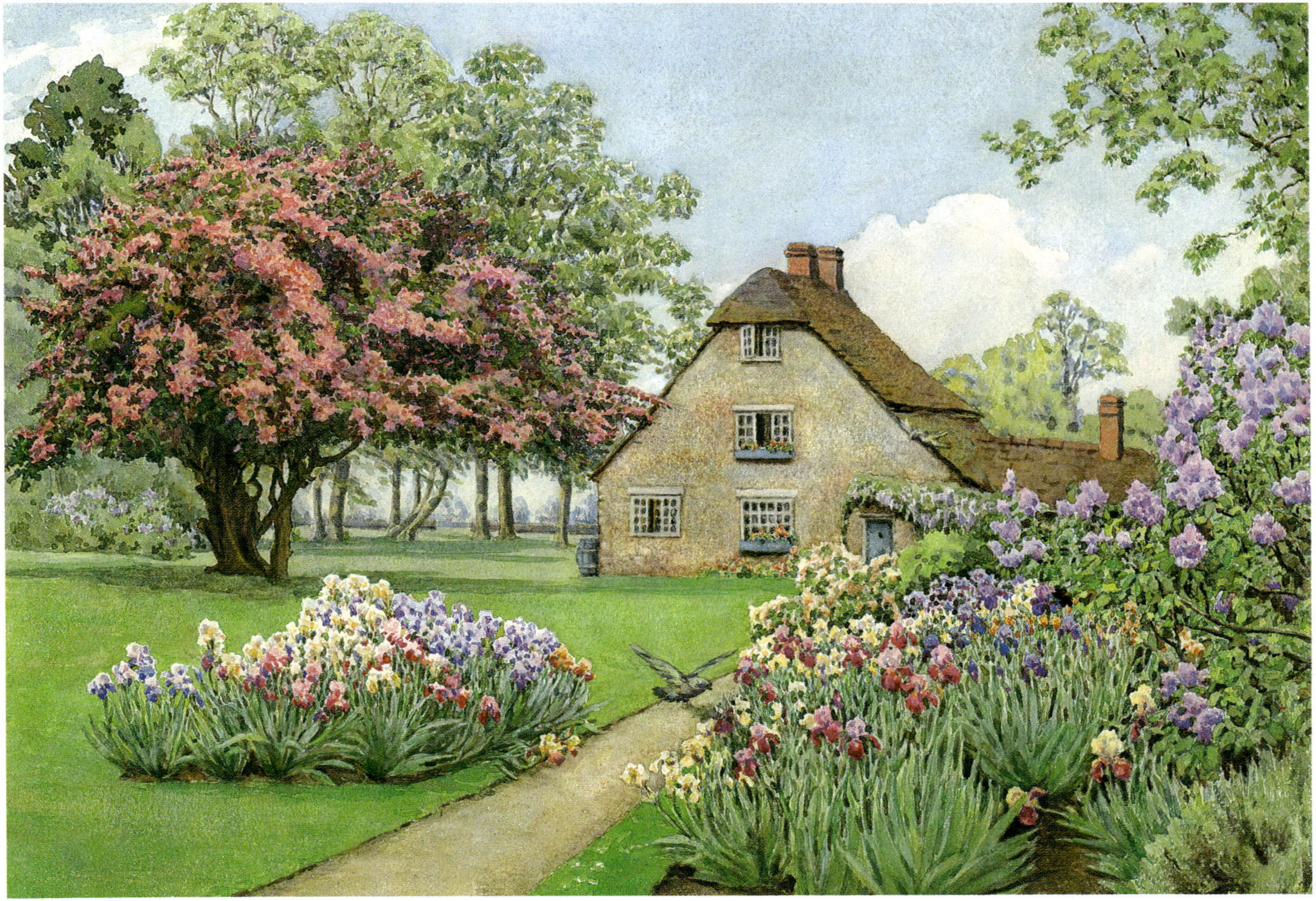

May Time by Nancy Dowson

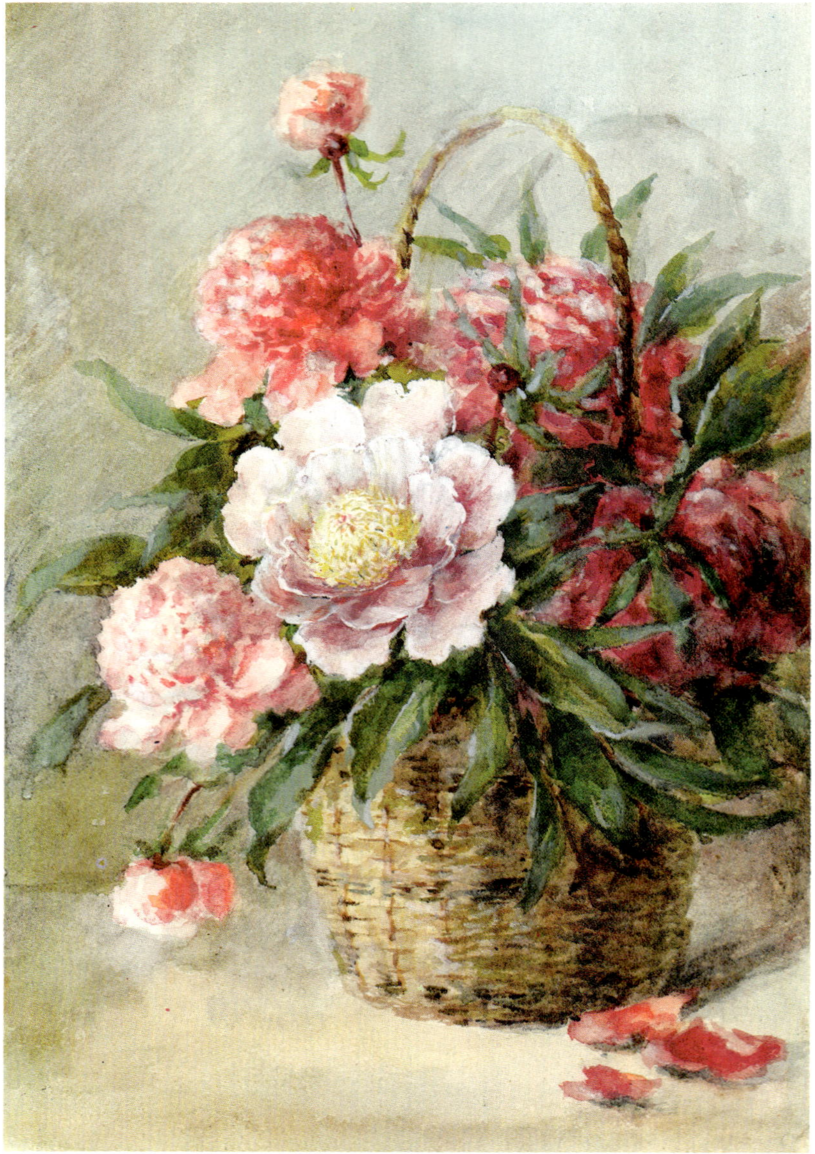

May I a small house, and a large
garden have!
And a few friends, and many books,
both true,
Both wise, and both delightful too!
And since Love ne'er will from
me flee,
A mistress moderately fair,
And good as guardian angels are,
Only beloved and loving me!

Abraham Cowley

Peonies by Annie L Pressland

HENRY JOHN SYLVESTER STANNARD was a watercolour painter of landscape, rustic and garden subjects; he was a member of a family of notable water-colour artists. His father, Henry Stannard was a painter of sporting subjects and three sisters and a brother also exhibited water-colour garden scenes and landscapes. Henry John, known to his friends as Harry, was born in 1870 in Bedford. He attended Bedford Modern School and studied art at South Kensington where he gained an art teacher's diploma at the age of sixteen. He painted loosely in the style of Birkett Foster and exhibited at the Royal Society of British Artists from 1890, at the Royal Academy and at numerous other galleries in London and the provinces. He was elected RBA in 1896. He died at Flitwick in Bedfordshire in January 1951.

Phlox drummondii and Verbena
by Annie L Pressland

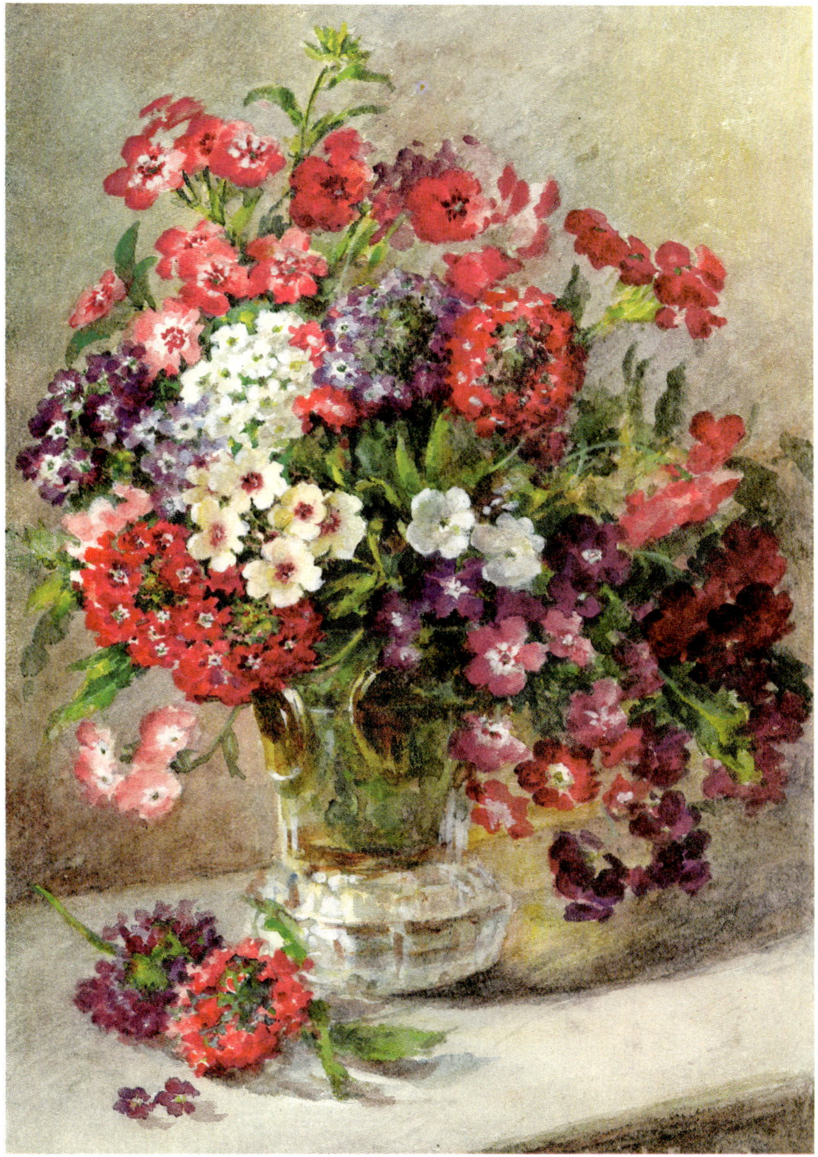

JULY

Given good weather what a month this is. The Sweet Peas and Delphiniums may need constant tying but they are worth all the attention we can give them. The Rambler Roses and many annuals in the borders should be at their best. Don't forget to keep the hoe going between the various plants, until the foliage and flower spikes meet. Watch the staking and tying and don't forget to thin the Asters or Michaelmas Daisy shoots; five to a plant is plenty. Keep the Begonias and Fuchsias mulched and moist; they don't like dry conditions. Stop your early flowering Chrysanthemums if they are inclined to run to flower too soon and support the Gladioli spikes. The Blackcurrants are ready and don't forget to cut out the old fruiting shoots once the crop is finished. As soon as you can, remove the Strawberry nets and layer strong young healthy plants for next year's planting. Use 60-sized pots if you can and loamy soil; never let them get dry. There are plenty of vegetables ready now. Keep the Tomatoes to one stem and stop at the fourth truss; mulch if possible. Get out the Winter Greens, Brussels Sprouts and Winter Broccoli as they become ready.

A July Border by William Carruthers Affleck

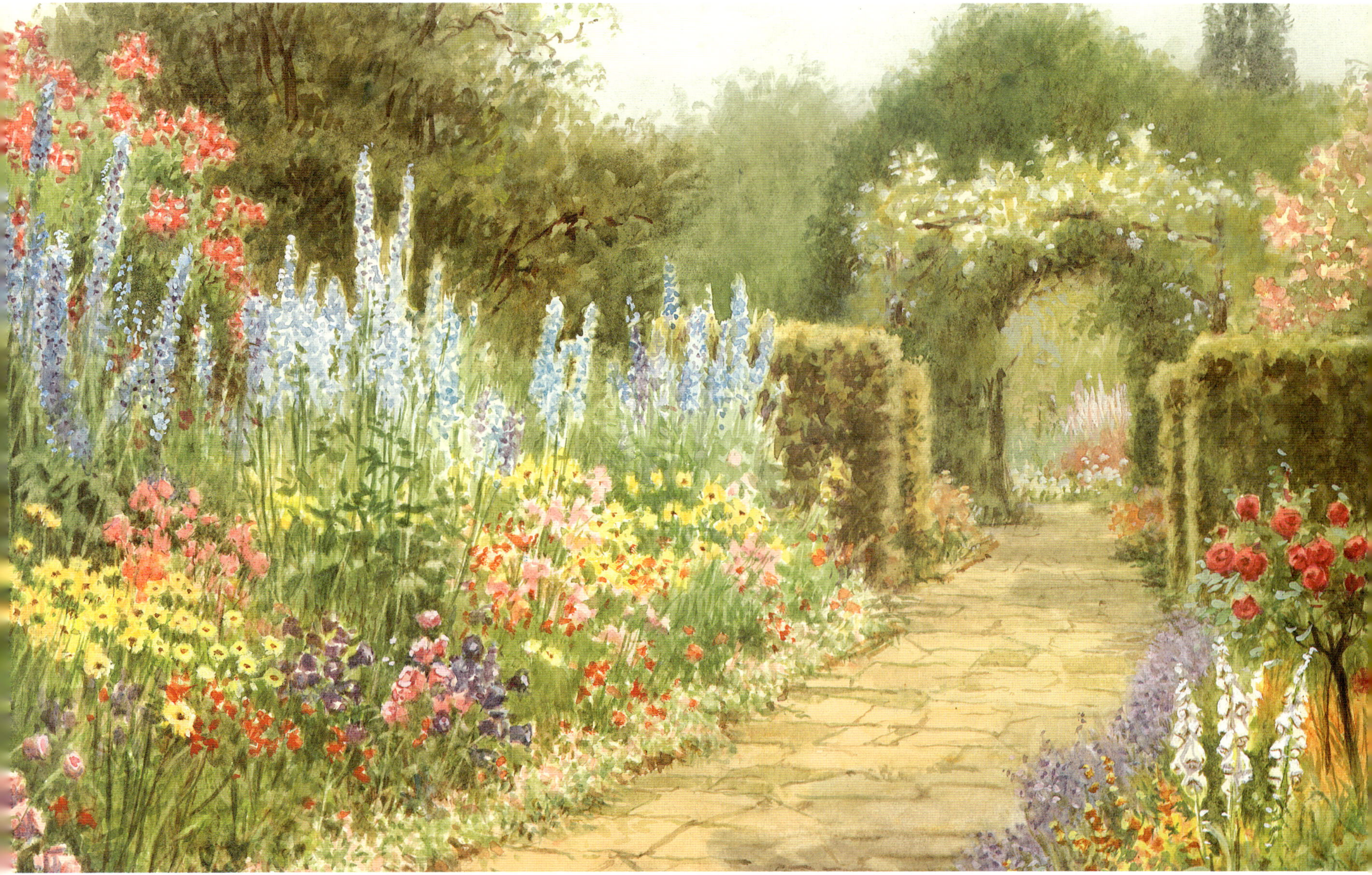

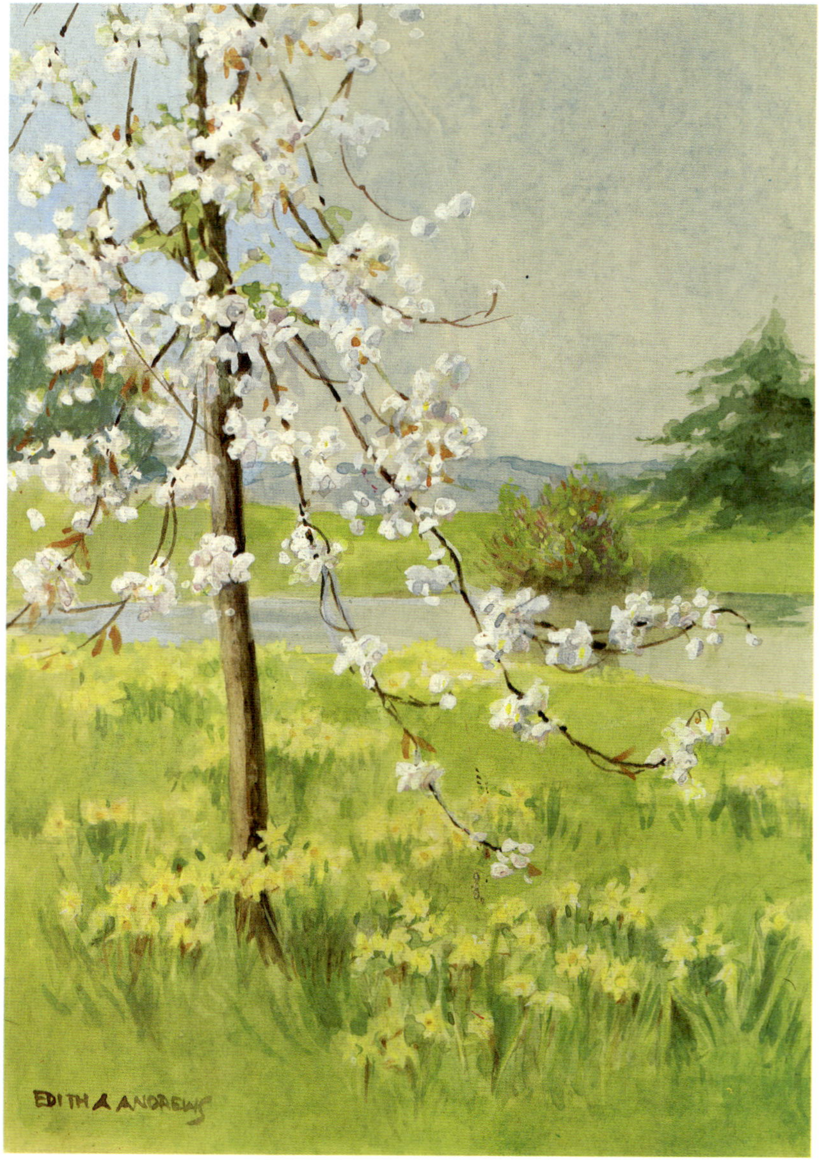

Loveliest of trees, the cherry now
Is hung with bloom along
the bough,
And stands about the woodland ride
Wearing white for Eastertide.
A E Houseman

Daffodils and Cherry
by Edith A Andrews

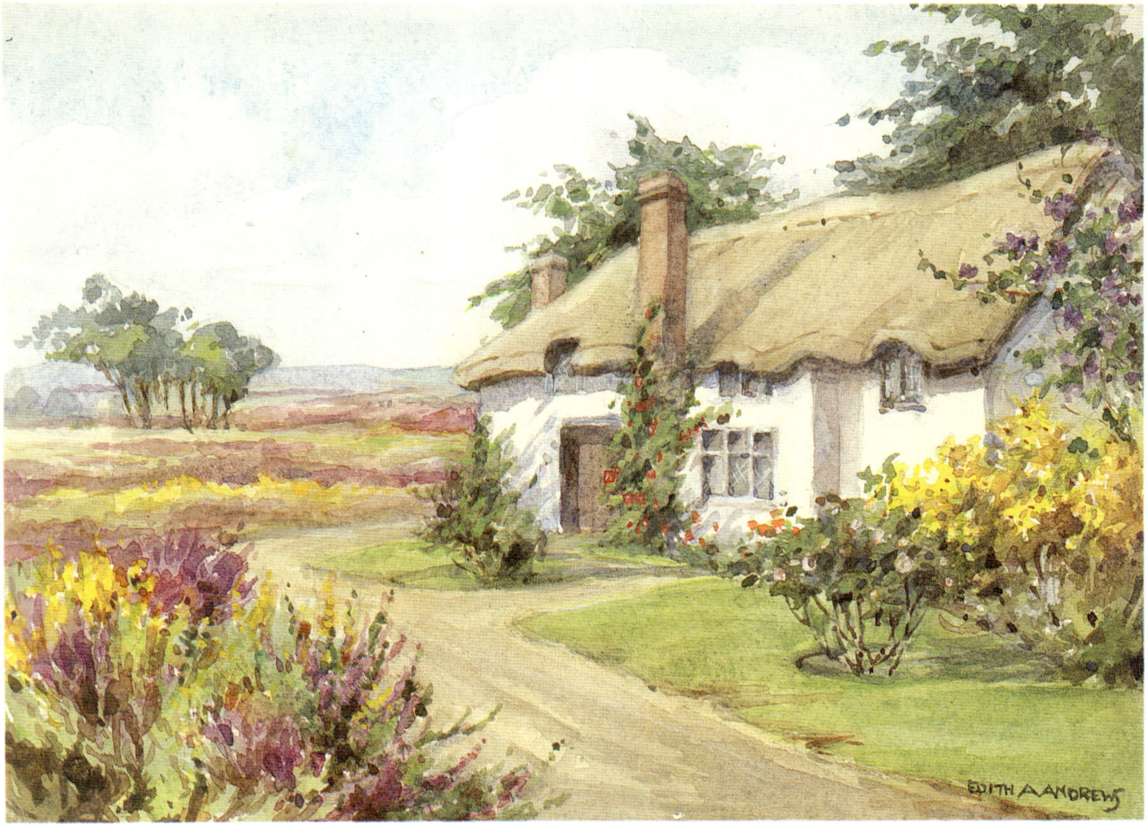

A Moorland Cottage by Edith A Andrews

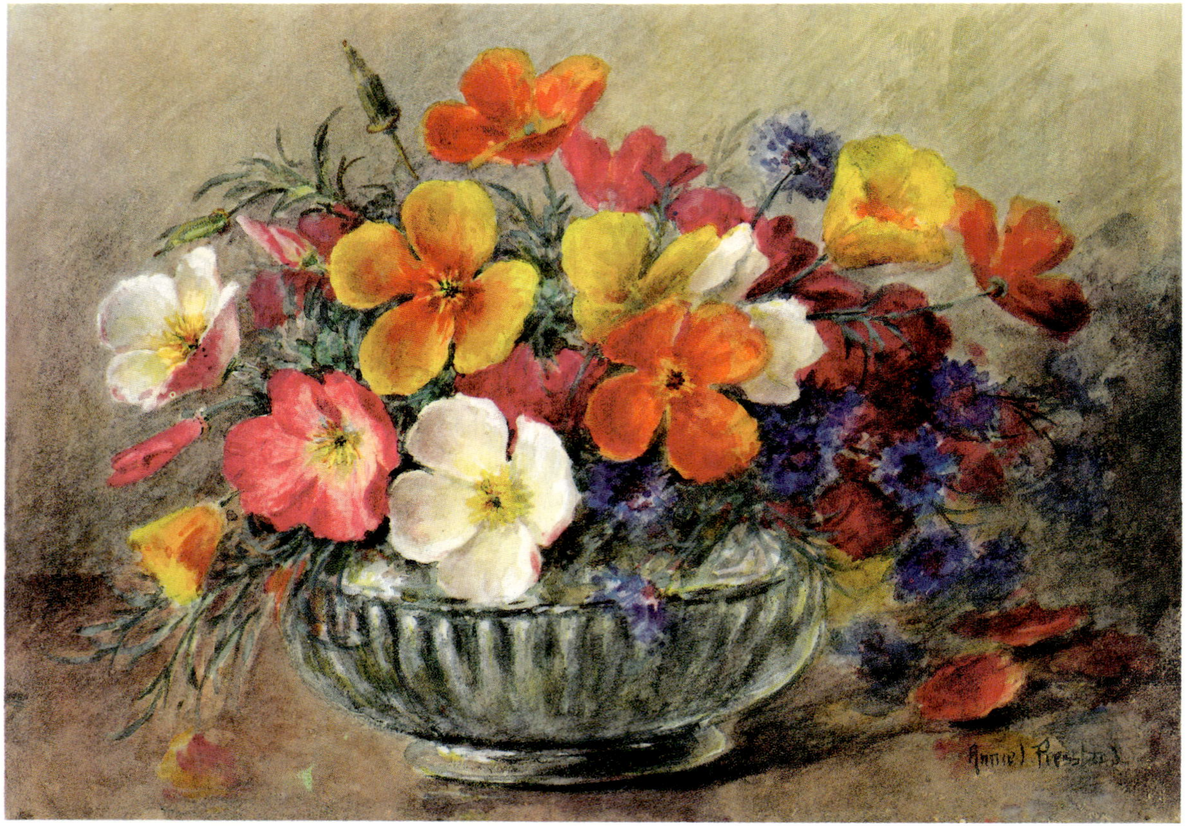

Eschscholtzias and Cornflowers by Annie L Pressland

THERESA SYLVESTER STANNARD was a watercolour painter of flowers, cottages, rustic scenes and gardens. She was born in 1898 at Flitwick near Bedford, the only child of Henry John Sylvester Stannard, RBA, and his first wife Annie. Theresa inherited her father's and her grandfather Henry Stannard's artistic talent and first exhibited at the Royal Academy in 1915 at the age of sixteen when she had the distinction of being the youngest exhibitor. Thereafter she exhibited many times during her career including at the Royal Academy, the Royal Institute of Painters in Watercolours and the Society of Women Artists and also in the provinces. Marrying to become Mrs Dyer she lived at 64 Spenser Road, Bedford, where she shared a studio with her father, who lived at Flitwick some ten miles from Bedford. She died in 1947.

Daffodils and Wallflowers
by Annie L Pressland

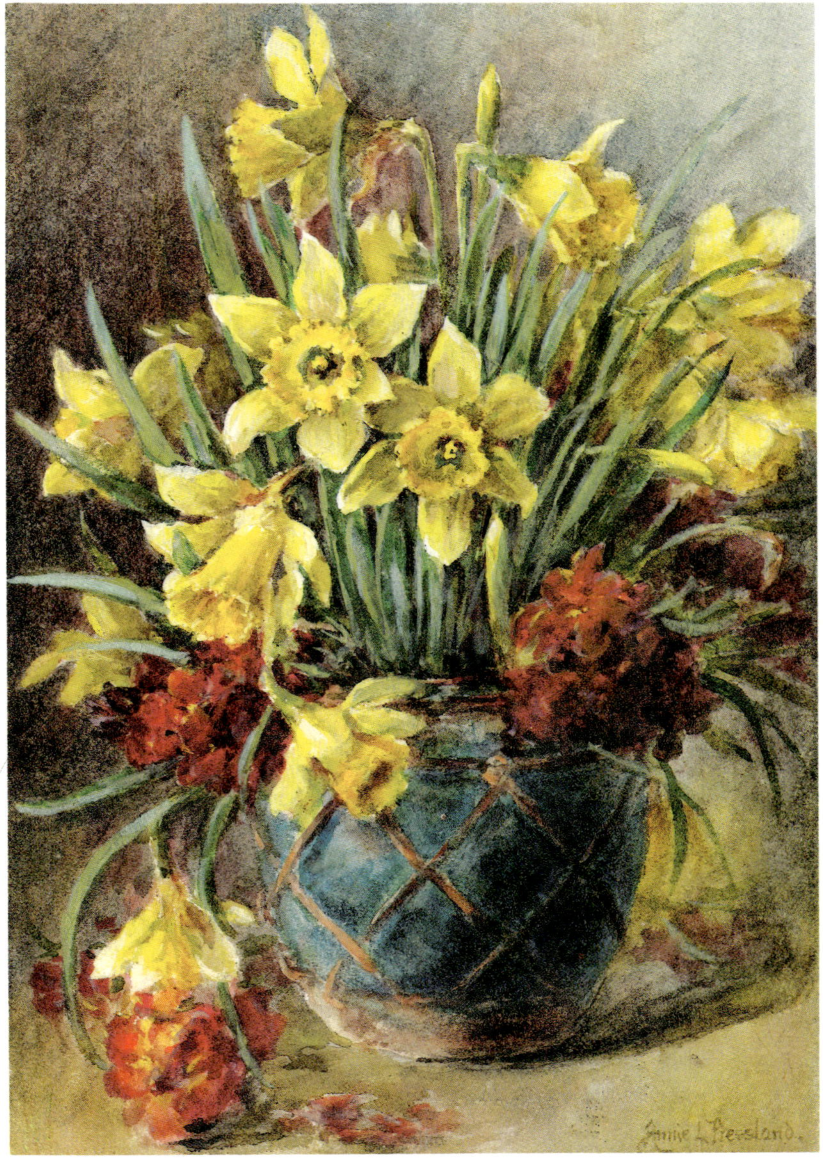

AUGUST

The fruits are now ripening. Eat those early Apples from the tree: don't try to store them, they are not meant to keep. Peach, Nectarines, Apricots and Plums all ripening and don't forget to cut out the old fruiting Raspberry canes once the fruit is picked. Plant your new Strawberry beds on well-manured ground and grow some of the new perpetual varieties, they go on fruiting until the frost comes. In the flower borders Dahlias are opening fast. Keep them nice and moist and always remove the dead flowers immediately; in fact that applies to all flowers. Start to take your Geranium cuttings, don't spoil the beds or plants, but a growth here and there. Prune the Rambler Roses once they are over. In the vegetable quarters keep everything sown up, mulched and watered; remember a dry plant is suffering and therefore not at it's best, either to eat or to look at.

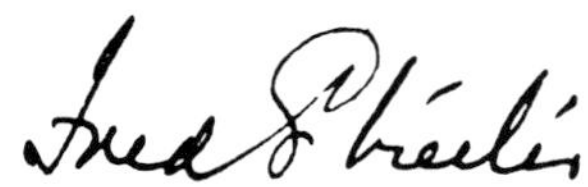

The Fountain by Theresa S Stannard

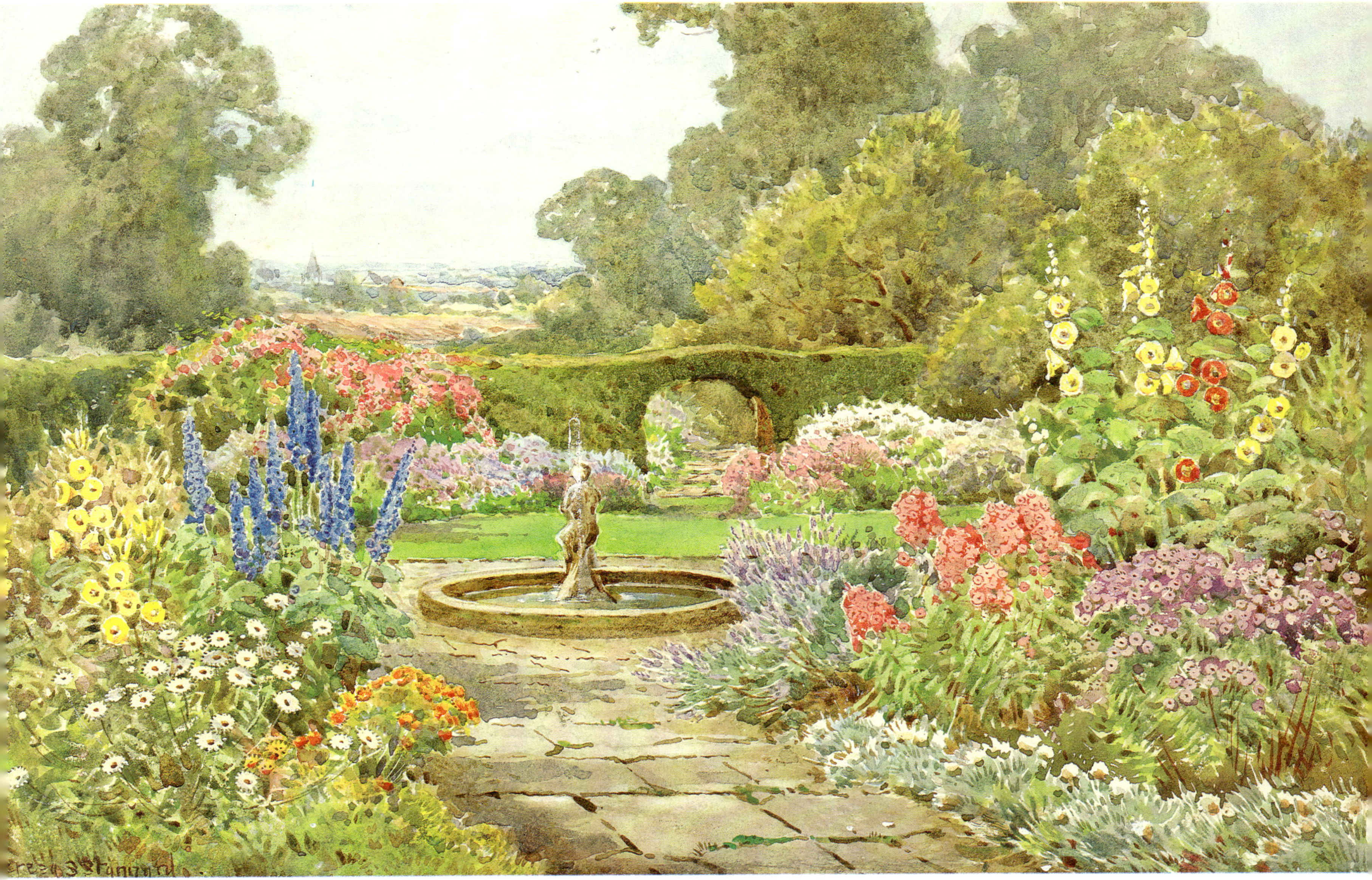

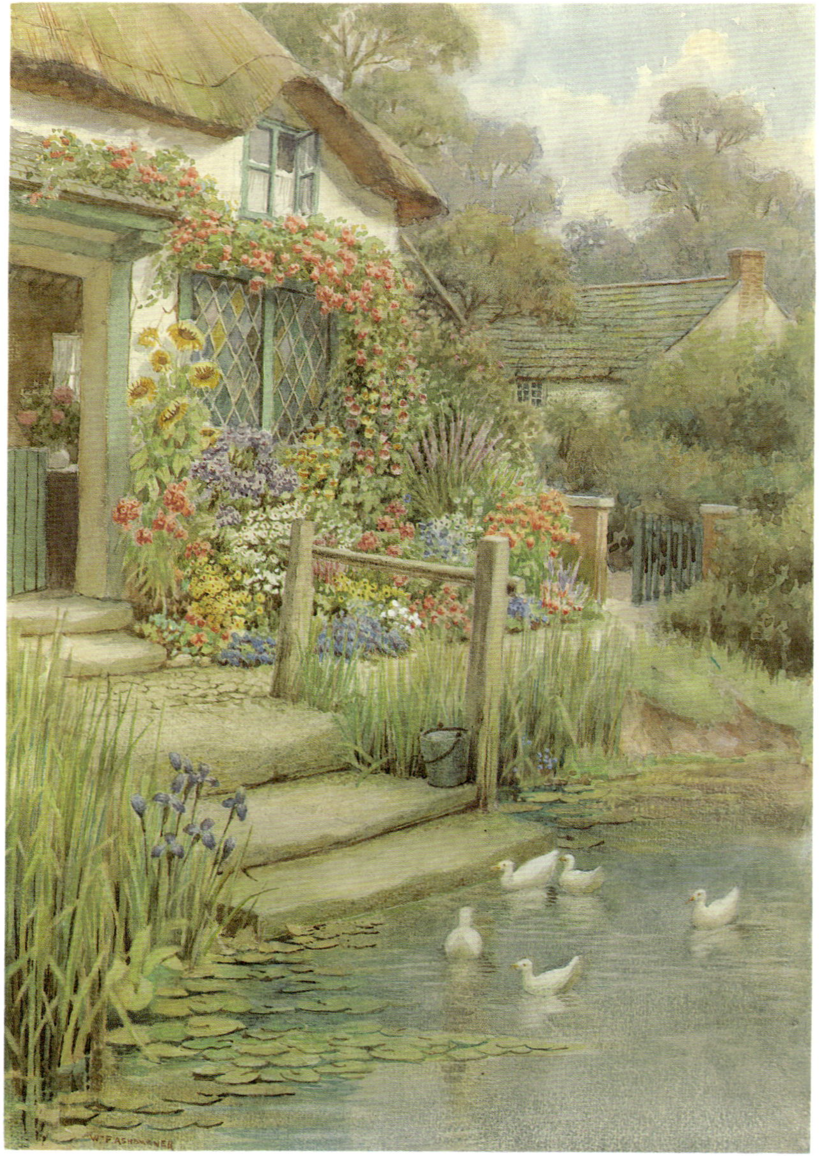

WILLIAM F ASHBURNER was a watercolour painter of gardens, cottages and genre subjects in a delicate, quiet and reflective style. He exhibited between 1900 and 1932 at the Royal Academy, the Royal Institute of Painters in Watercolours, the Royal Scottish Academy and at a number of provincial galleries. He lived at 71 Priory Road, Kew until 1927 when he moved to Elmlea, West Street, Ewell, Surrey where he remained until his death in 1940.

Beside the Stream
by William F Ashburner

Mid pleasures and palaces though
we may roam
Be it ever so humble, there's no
place like home;
A charm from the sky seems to
hallow us there
Which, seek through the world, is
ne'er met with elsewhere.
Home, home, sweet, sweet home!
There's no place like home!

John Howard Payne

The Cottage Steps
by William F Ashburner

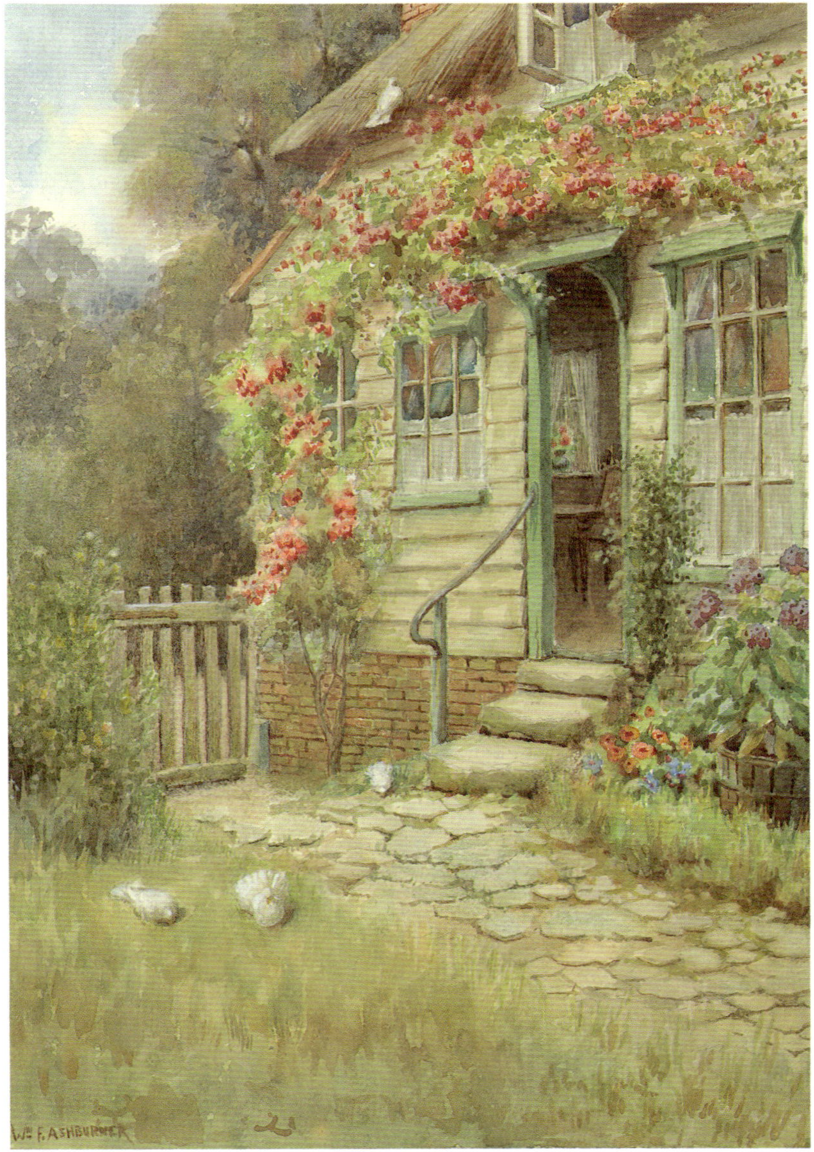

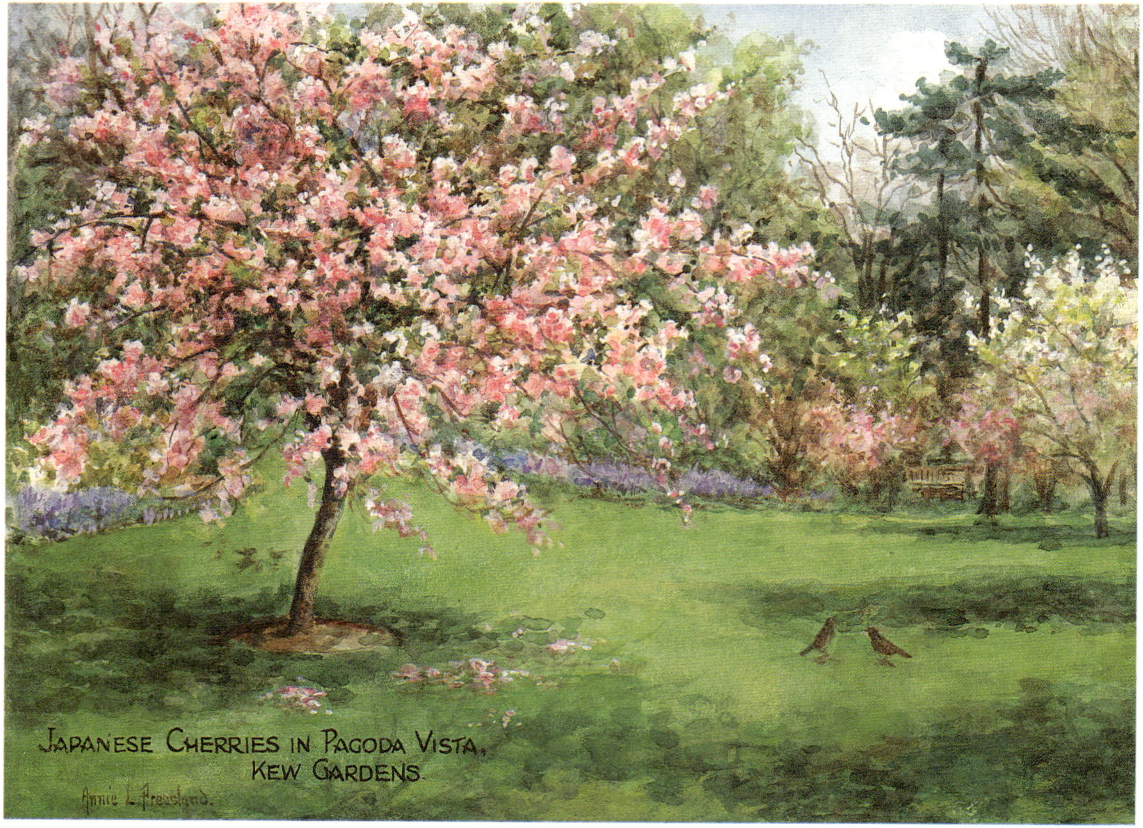

Japanese Cherries at Kew by Annie L Pressland

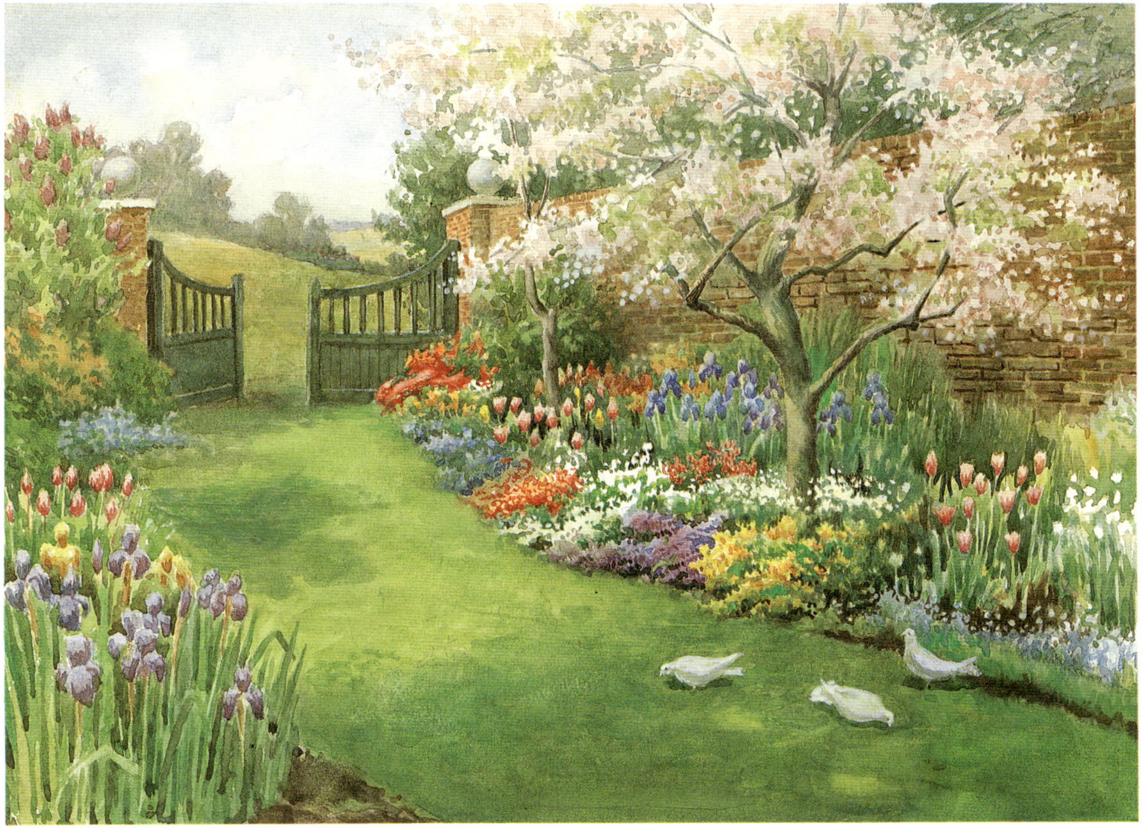

Tulip Time by William F Ashburner

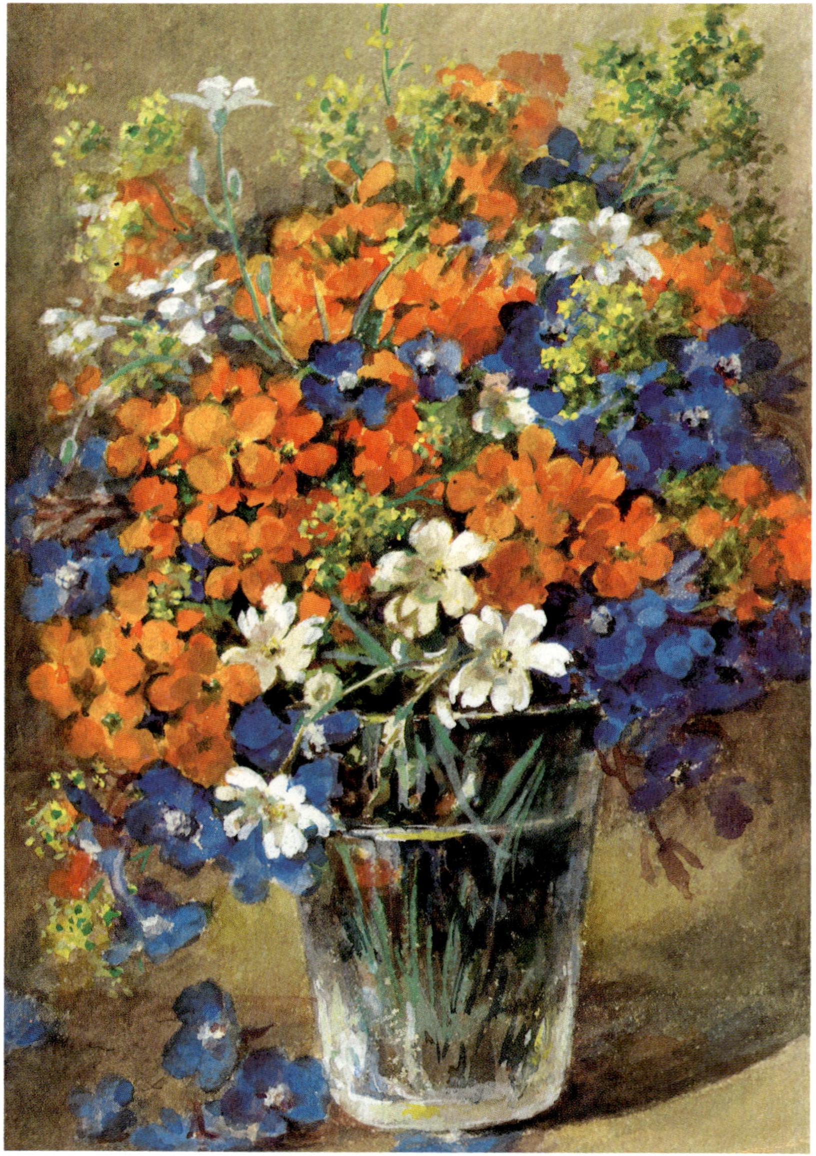

The Infinite has sowed his name in the heavens in burning stars, but on the earth he has sowed his name in tender flowers.

Jean Paul Richter

Siberian Wallflowers and Anchusa
by Annie L Pressland

Habits and customs differ,
but all peoples have the
love of flowers in common.
Chinese proverb

Anemone fulgens and Jonquils
by Annie L Pressland

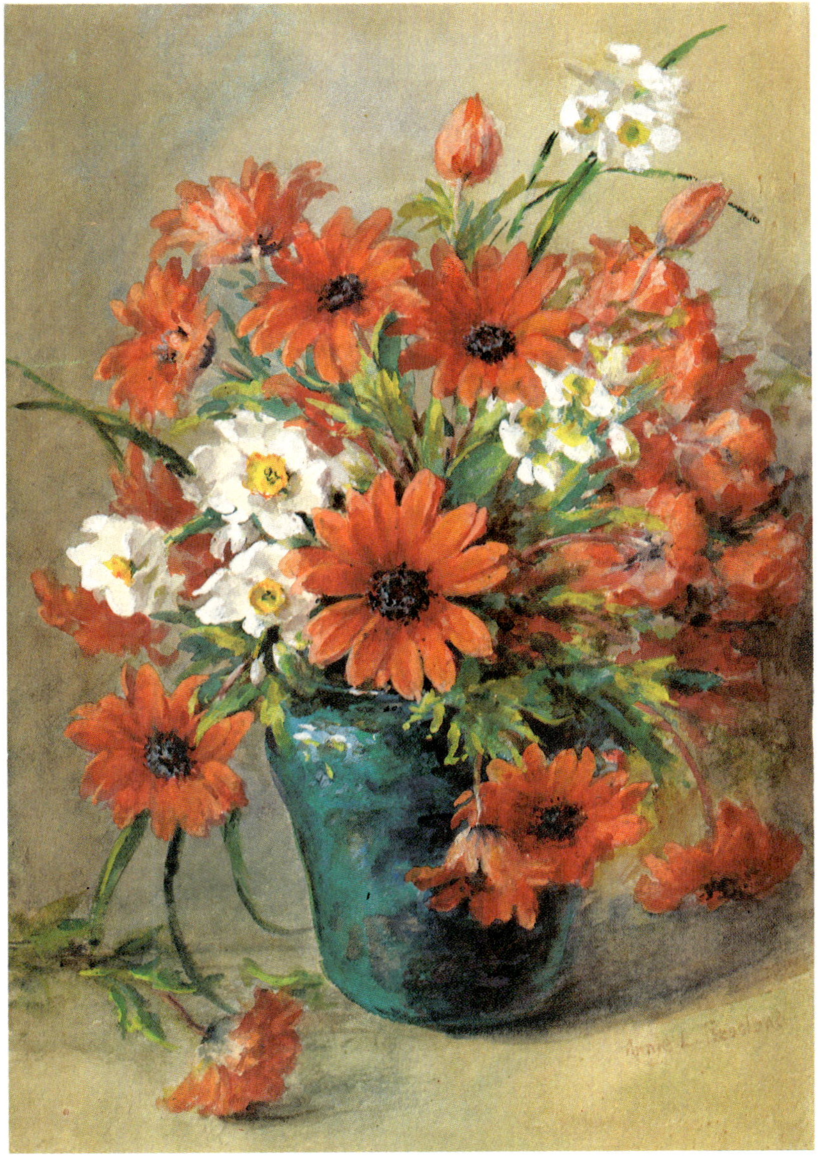

SEPTEMBER

This is the month for harvesting and preparing for another season. First the Onions are ready for lifting; always handle them carefully and lift with a garden fork – don't rely on pulling them by the neck. Let them stay on the ground for two or three days, then remove to the shed and await a wet day to clean and store them. Potatoes once they are finished are far better lifted and stored; again handle carefully. Get all the vacant ground cropped with Winter Greens; a large sowing with green topped Turnips and Spinach. Earth the Celery, four inches at a time. Plant out the Spring Cabbage and Endives and Winter Lettuce and sow Black Spanish and China Rose Radishes. Only pick your Apples and Pears when they are fit; Apples when the pips are brown, Pears when they part easily by an upward lift of the hand and always store Pears with the stalk uppermost. Keep the Dahlias going until the frost comes by keeping every dead flower picked out. Make certain your Geranium cuttings are rooted, together with all the other flowers that need yearly propagation. Watch for frosts towards the end of the month.

The Garden, Penshurst Place, Kent by C Essenhigh Corke

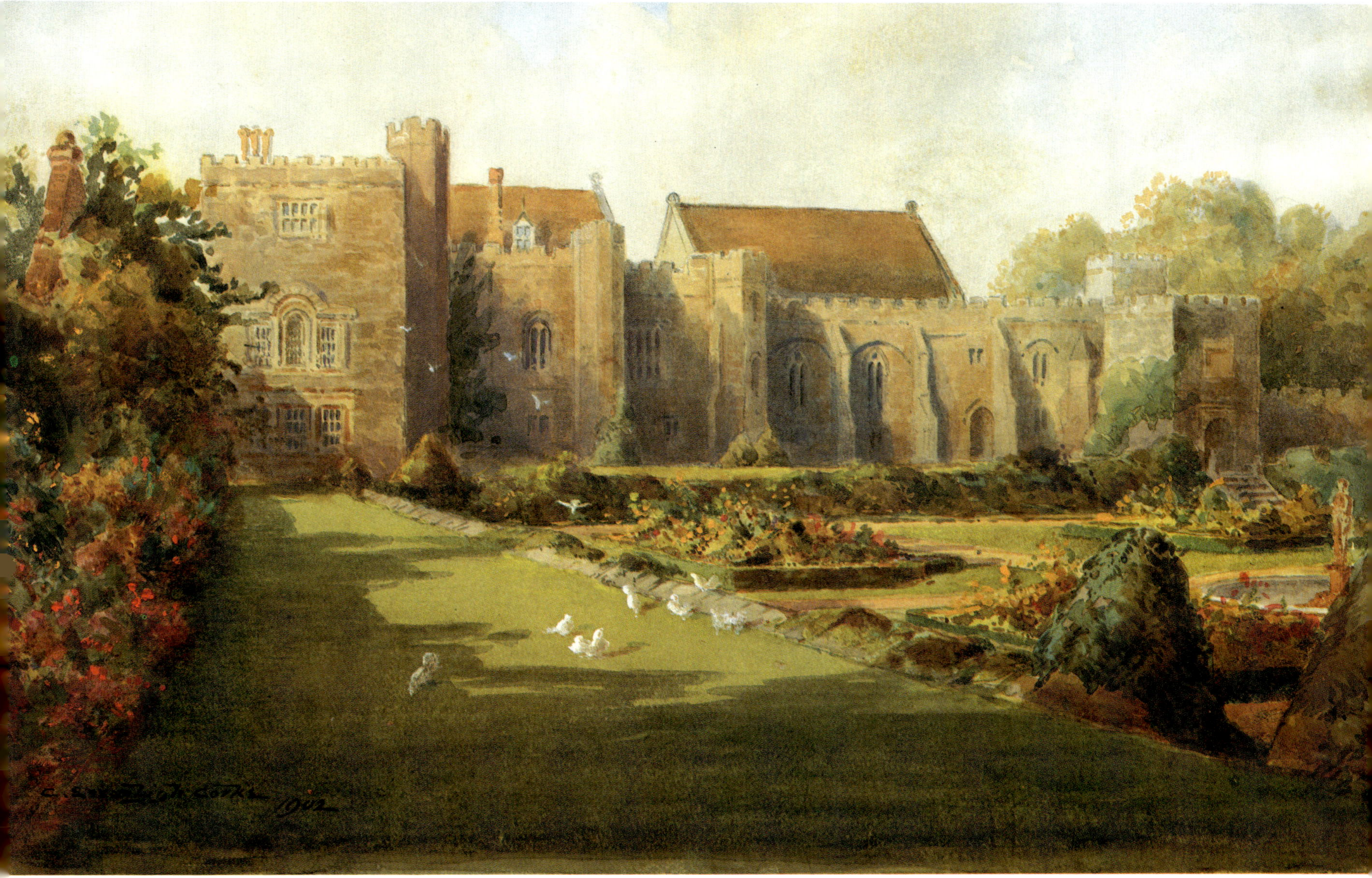
1902

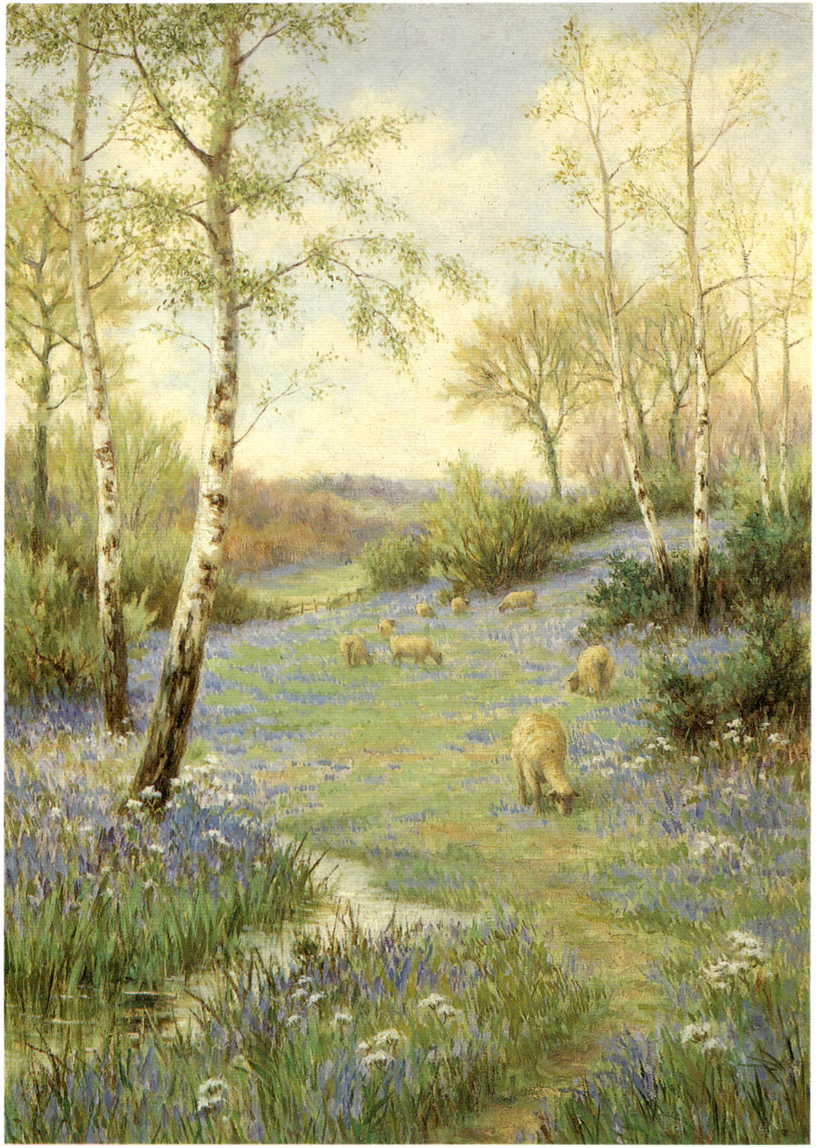

Gentle Spring! – in sunshine clad,
Well dost thou thy power display!
For Winter maketh the light
heart sad,
And thou, – thou makest the sad
heart gay.

Charles d'Orléans

A Bluebell Glade
by W Graham Buxton

The kiss of the sun for pardon,
The song of the birds for mirth,
One is nearer God's Heart
    in a garden,
Than anywhere else on earth.
Dorothy Gurney

The Well by James Matthews

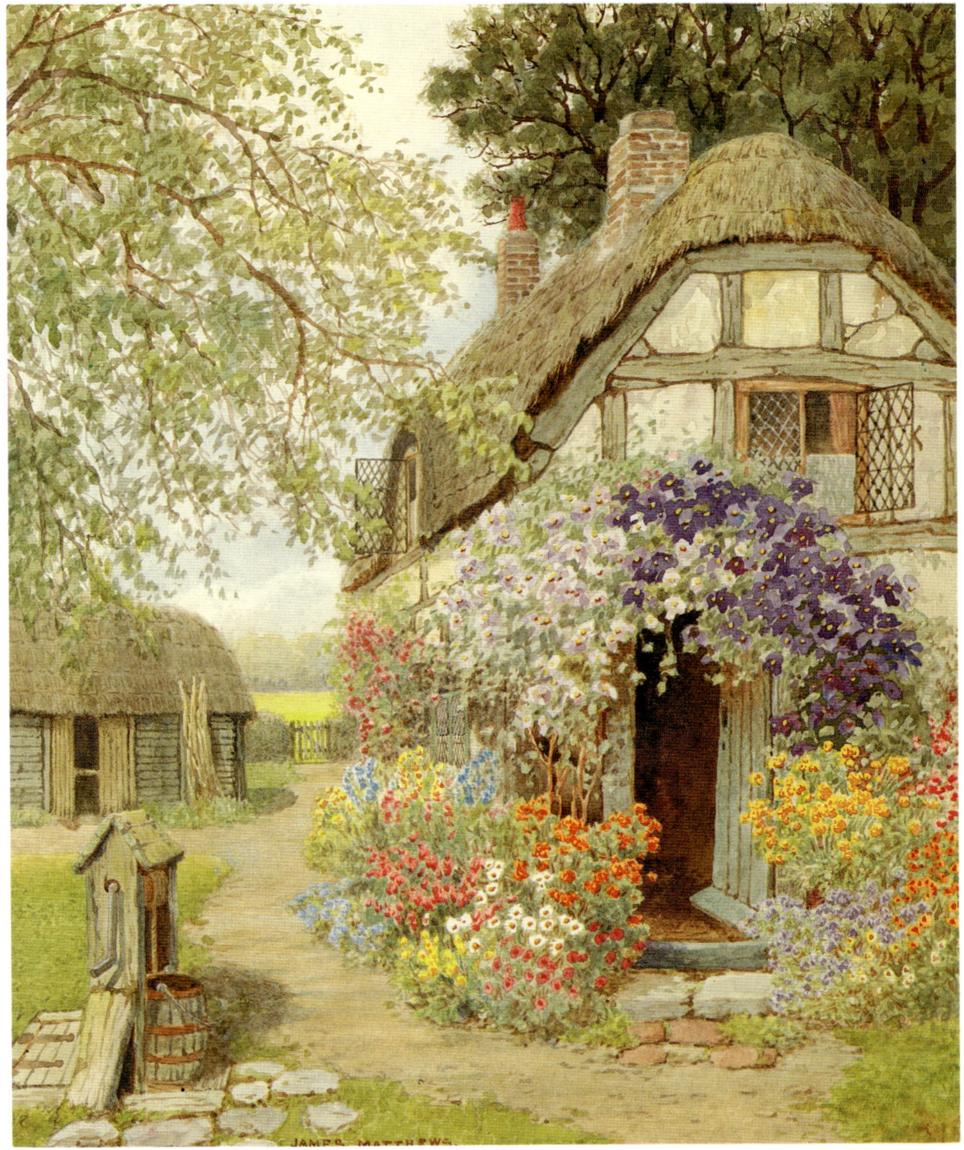

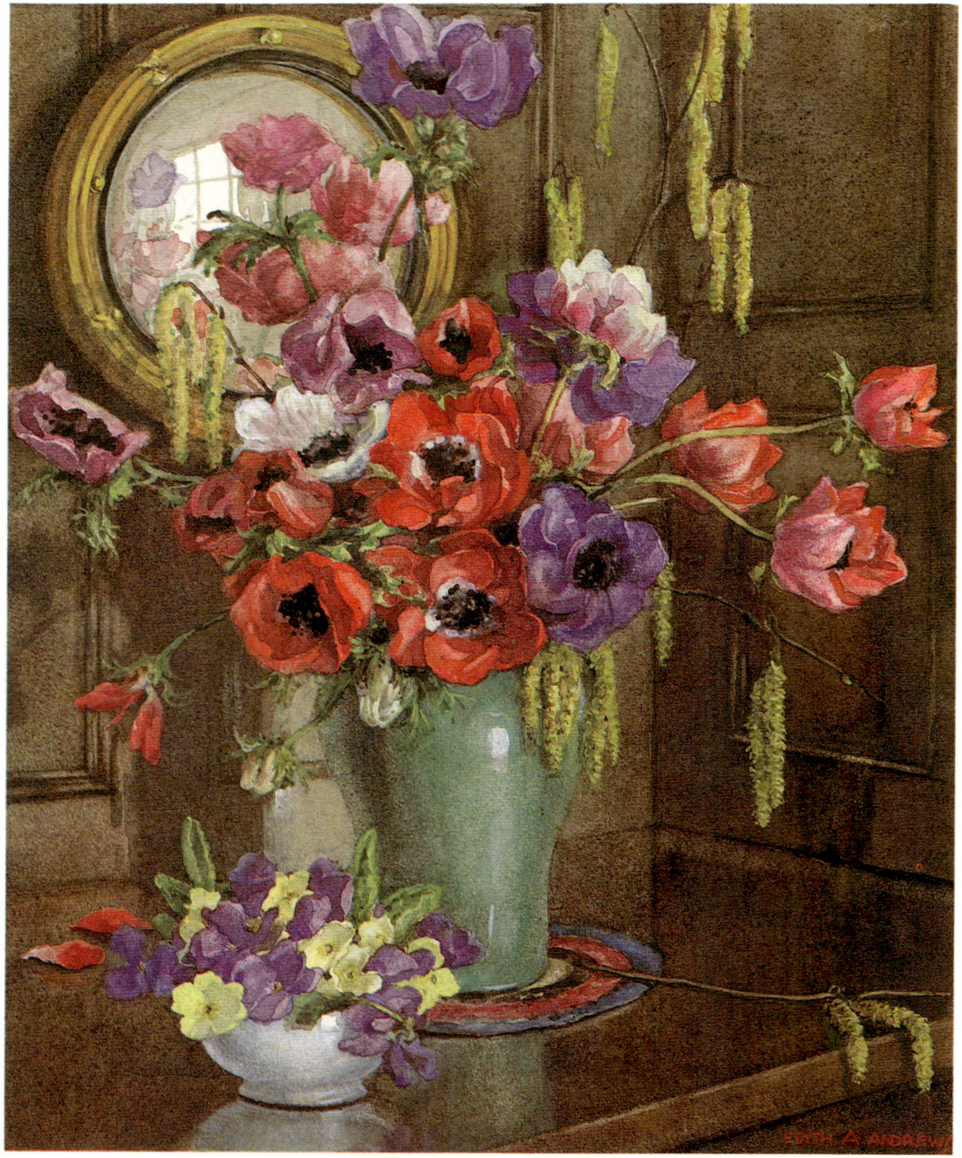

They speak of hope to the fainting
heart,
With a voice of promise they come
and part,
They sleep in dust through the
wint'ry hours,
They break forth in glory – bring
flowers, bright flowers!

Mrs F D Hemans

Spirit of Spring by Edith A Andrews

Not one of Flora's brilliant race
A form more perfect can display;
Art could not feign
more simple grace
Nor Nature take a line away.

James Montgomery

Narcissi and Anemones
by Edith A Andrews

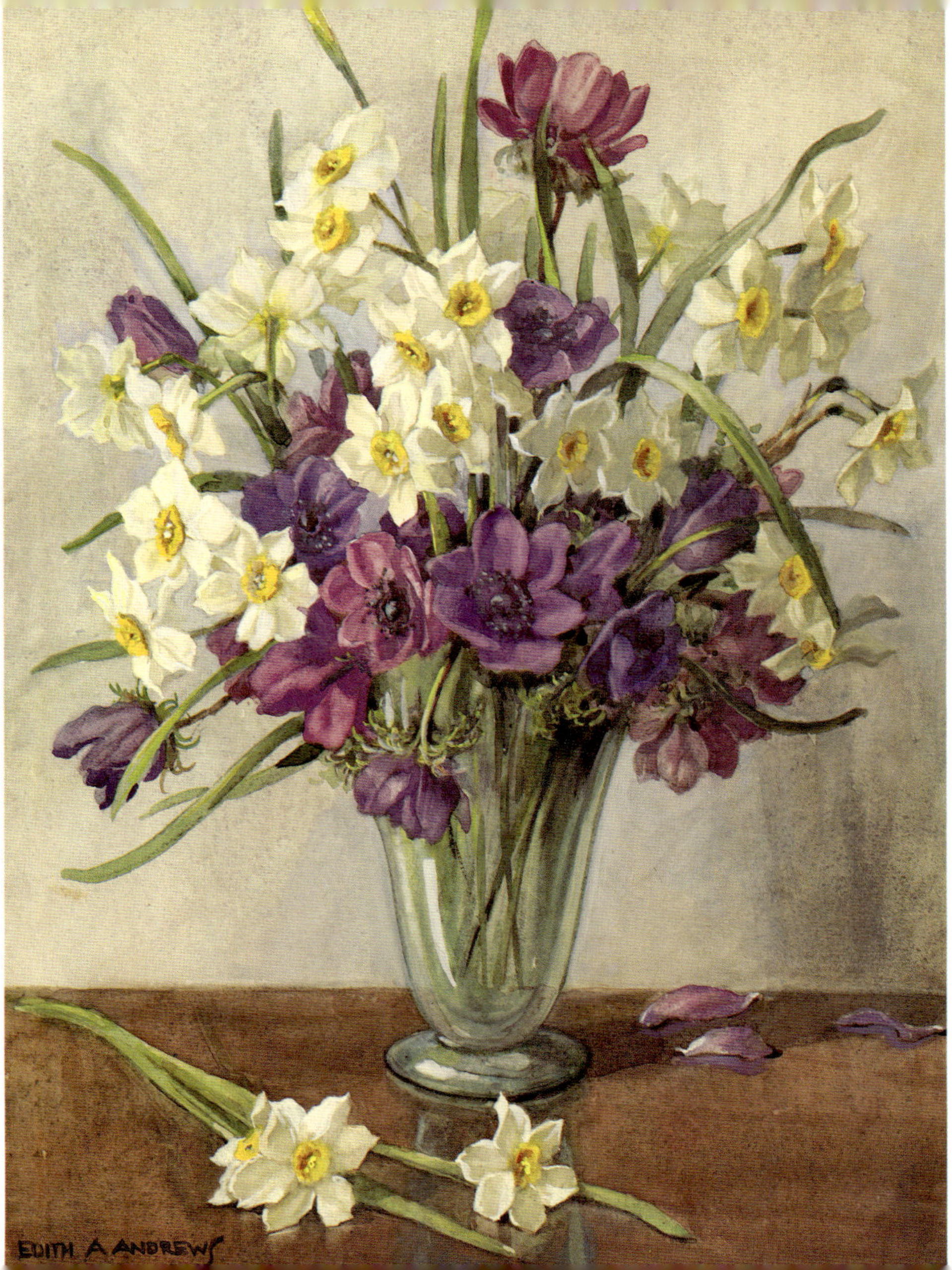

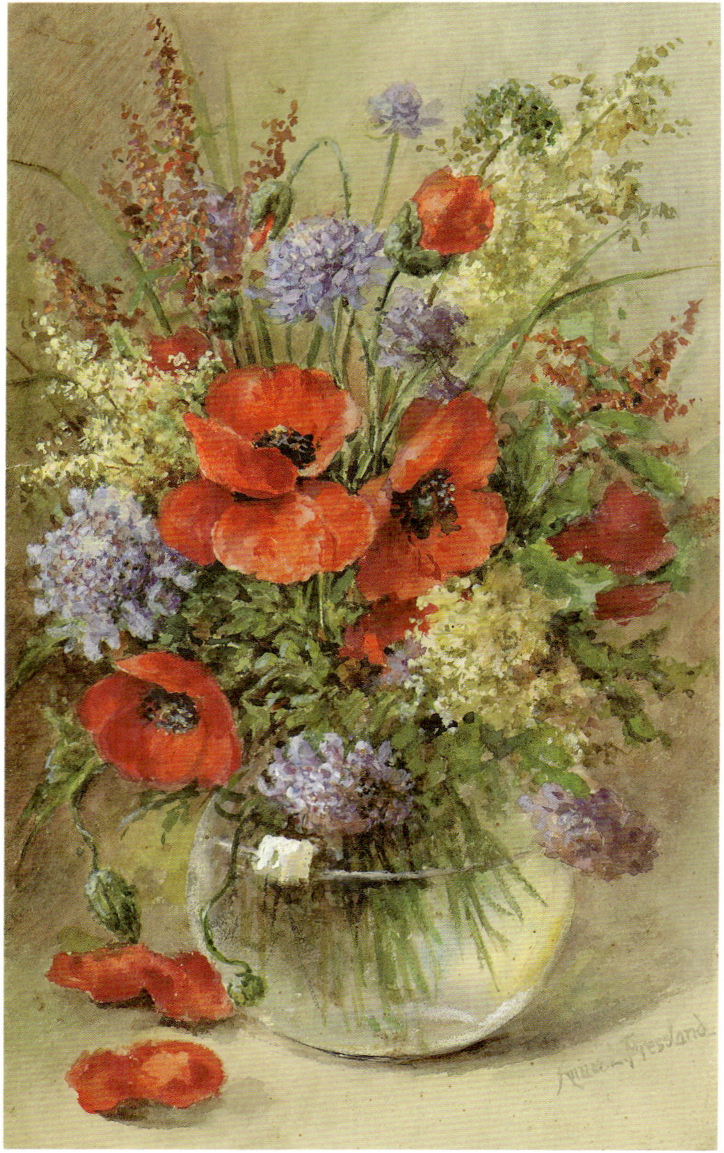

Summer set lip to earth's
bosom bare,
And left the flushed print in a
poppy there:
Like a yawn of fire from the grass
it came,
And the fanning wind puffed it to
flapping flame.
Francis Thompson

Poppies, Scabious and Meadowsweet
by Annie L Pressland

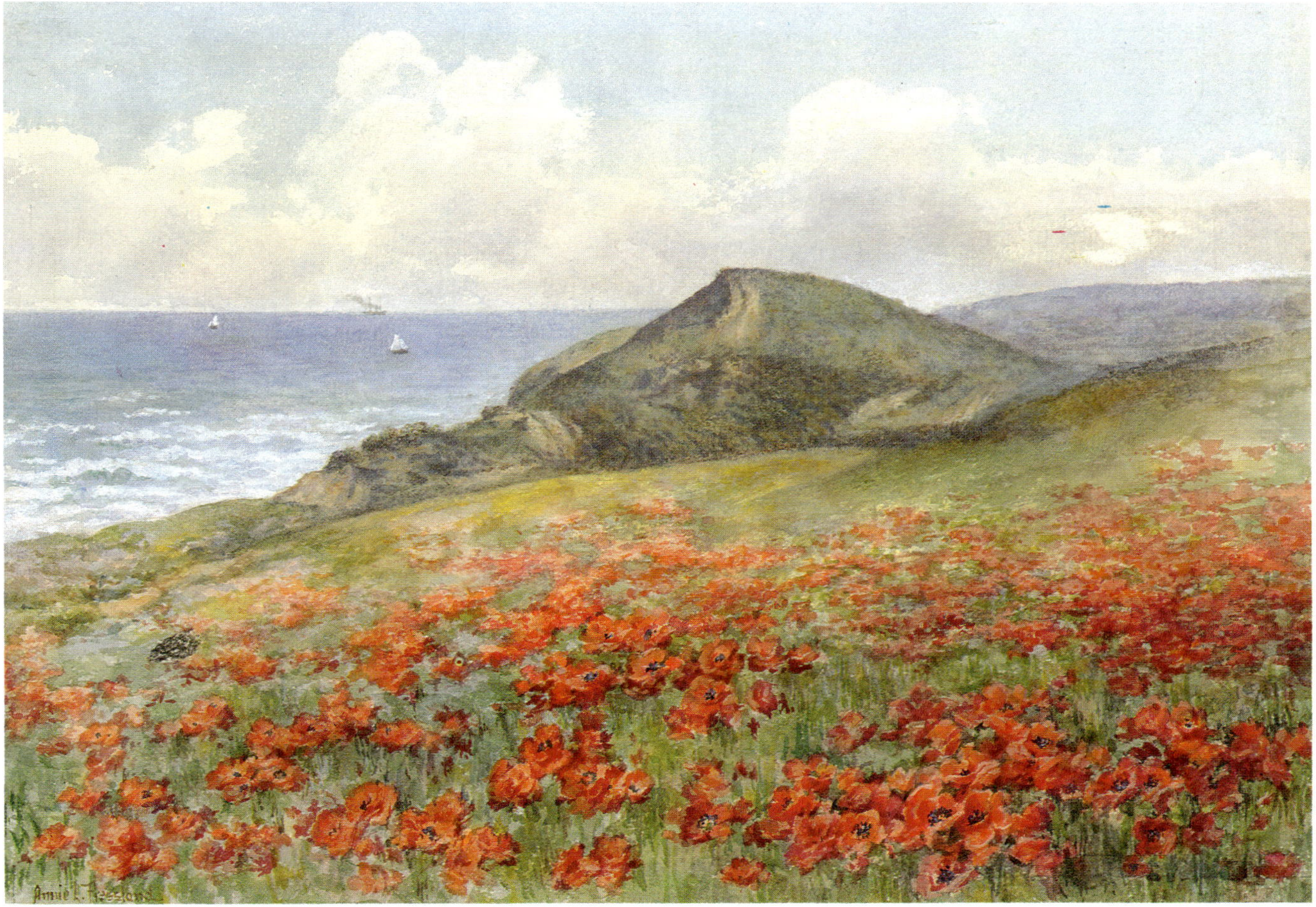

Poppyland by Annie L Pressland

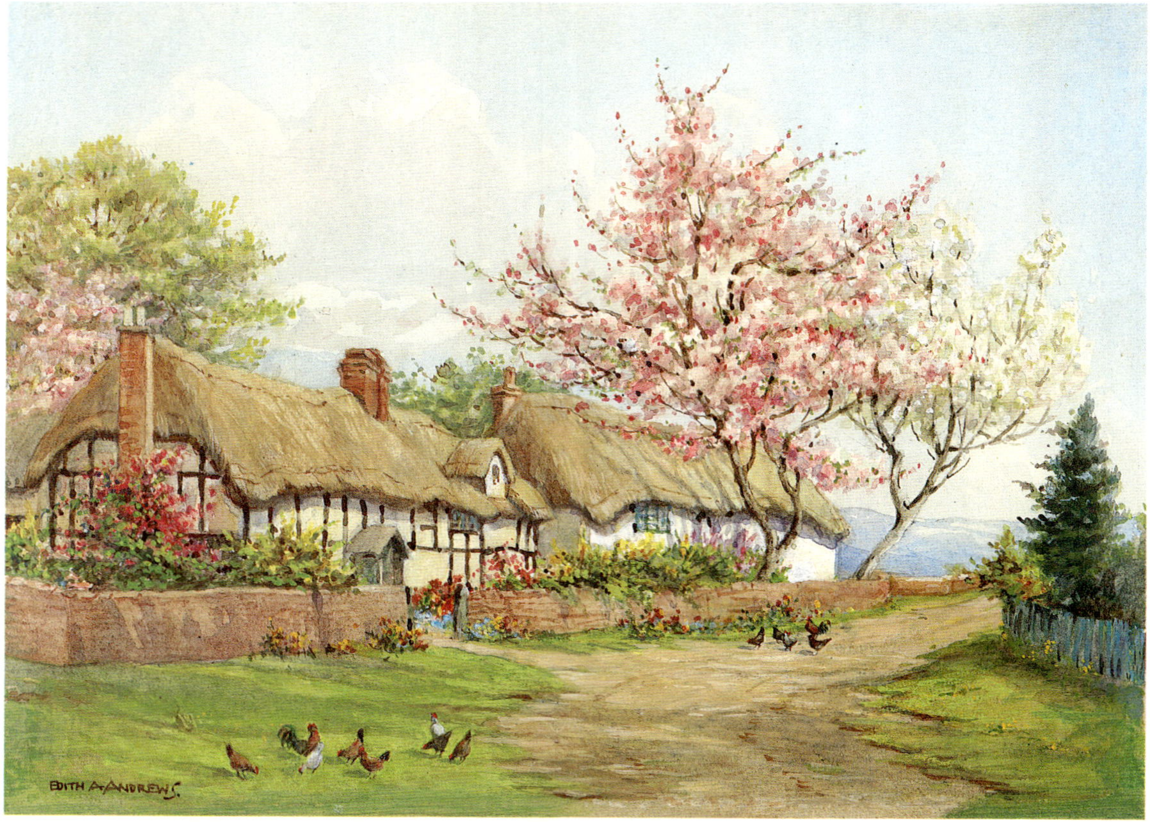

A Herefordshire Cottage by Edith A Andrews

Now rings the woodland loud
    and long,
The distance takes a lovelier hue,
And drowned in yonder living blue
The lark becomes a sightless song.
Alfred Lord Tennyson

*Birches and Bluebells
by Edith A Andrews*

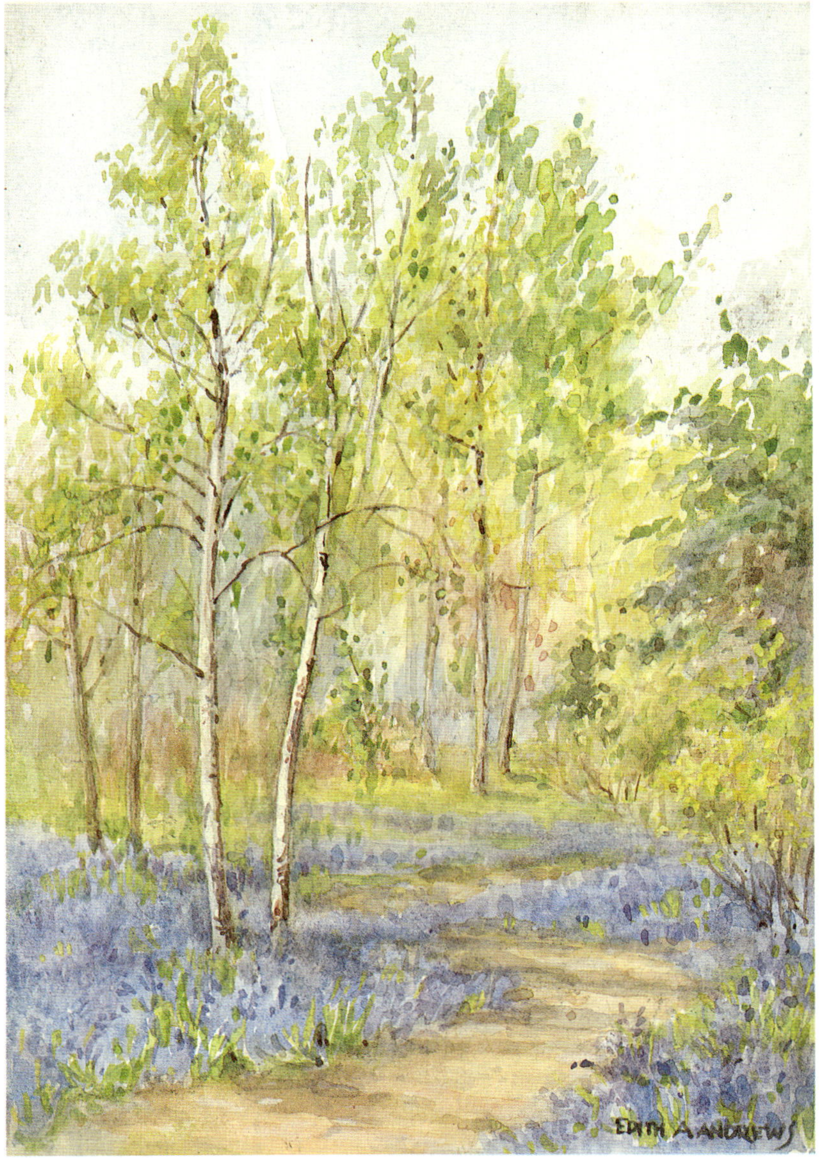

OCTOBER

Really the start to a Gardener's year in the flower garden. First get all the Christmas and forcing bulbs potted up; keep them plunged out of doors for the first six weeks, to get them thoroughly rooted first. Plant Wallflowers, Polyanthus and Forgetmenots in the beds to take the place of the Summer bedding; always plant firmly and get all bulbs planted if possible; make sure they are on a firm base. If not already done, take out all the old, flowering shoots of Rambling Roses and tie in the new growth. Order new Roses to be sent when they're lifted. The main Apple and Pear crop are now ready. Handle very carefully at all times, keep the store-house floor damp and never store on hay or straw, it may taint them. Leave the long-keeping sorts till the very last; don't pick them too soon. Continue to earth up the Celery. Make sure all the crops that are matured are lifted and stored. Draw a little soil up to the Spring Cabbages planted last month. Put Lettuce, Endives and Parsley into frames for Winter work.

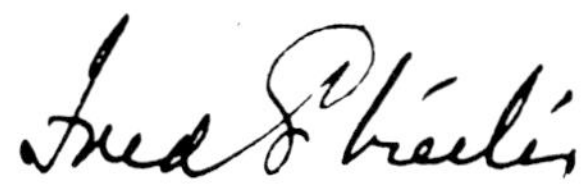

The Boathouse by Theresa S Stannard

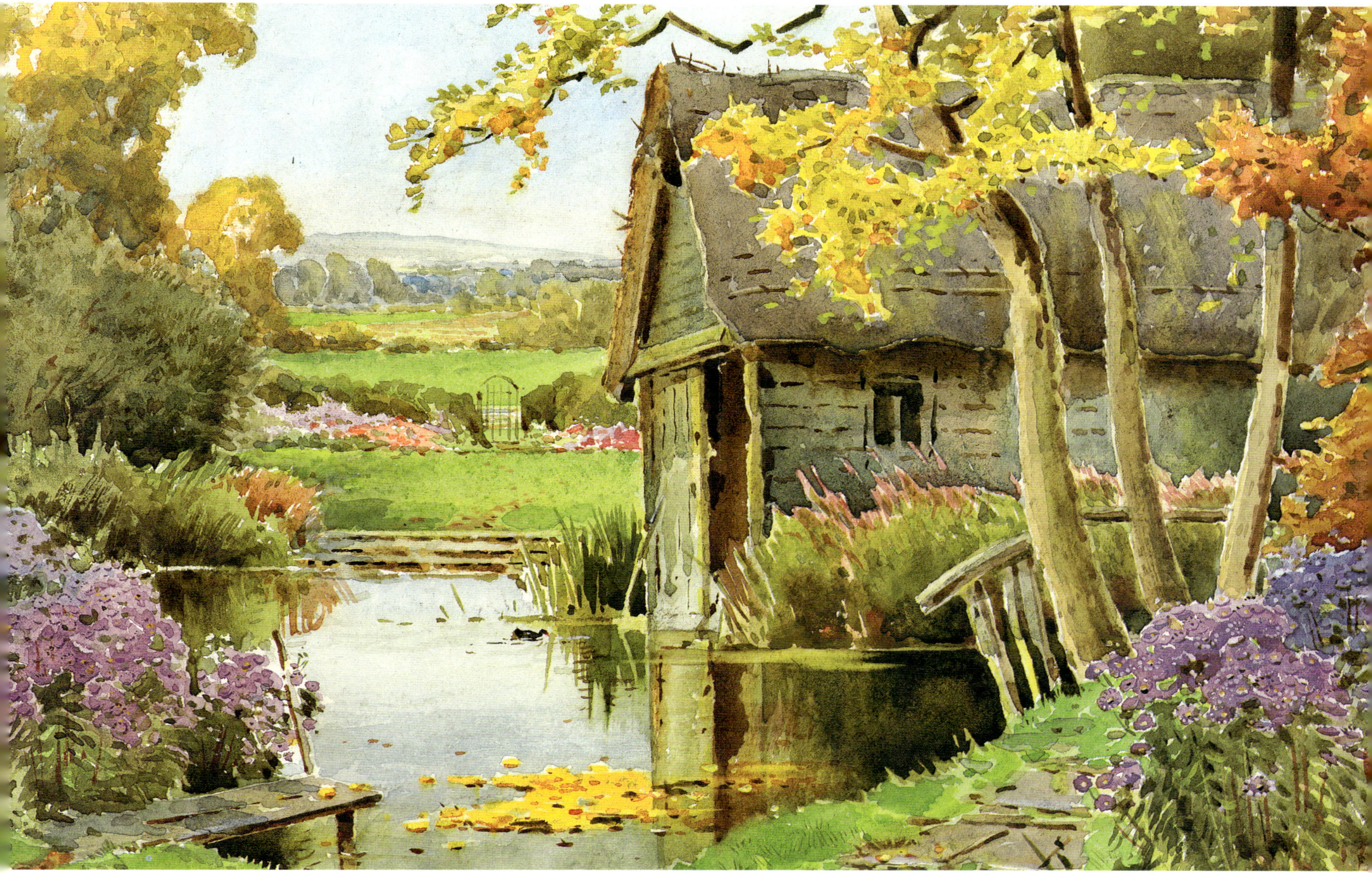

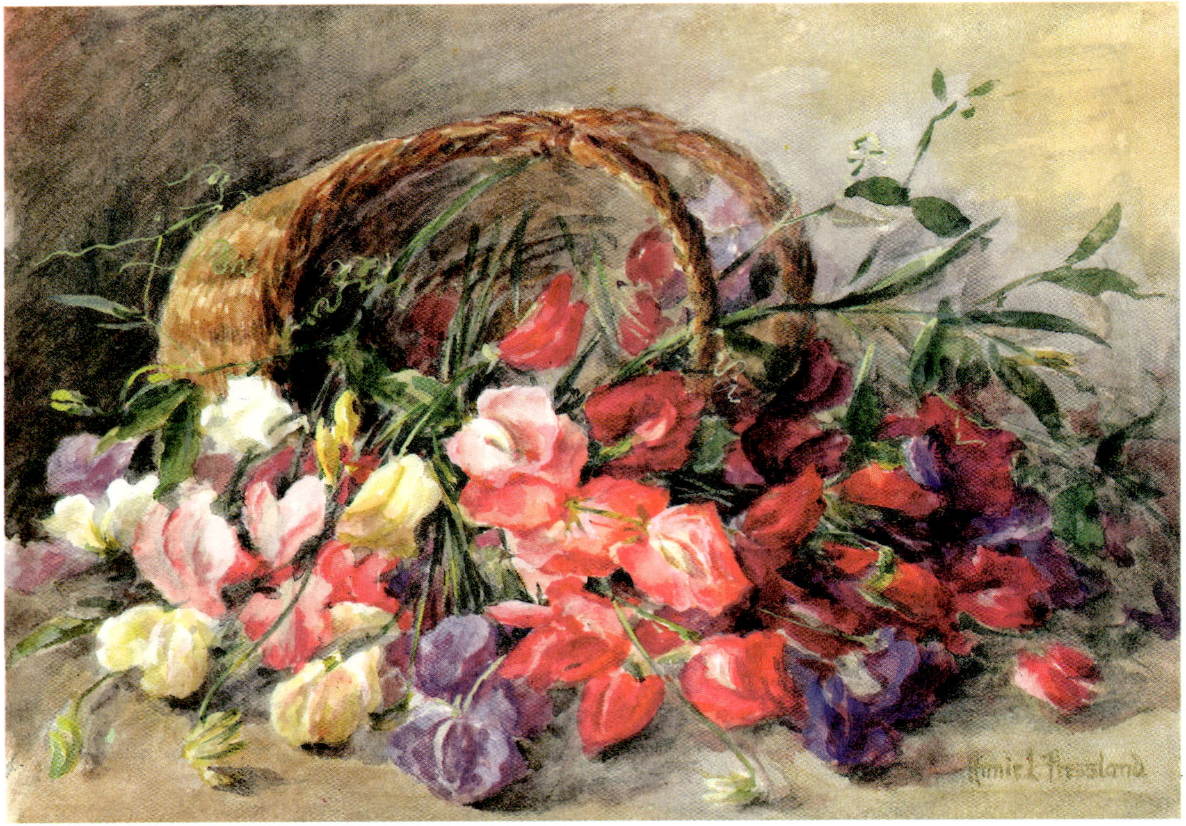

Sweet Peas by Annie L Pressland

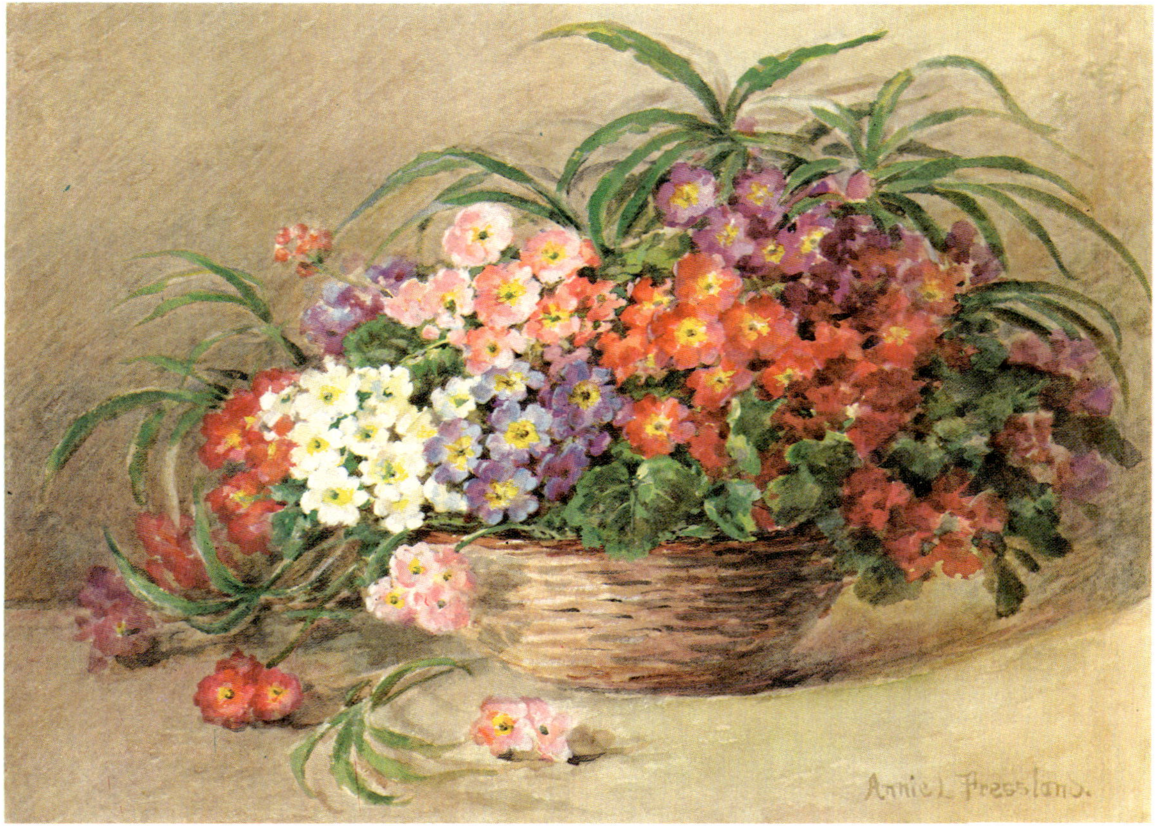

Primulas by Annie L Pressland

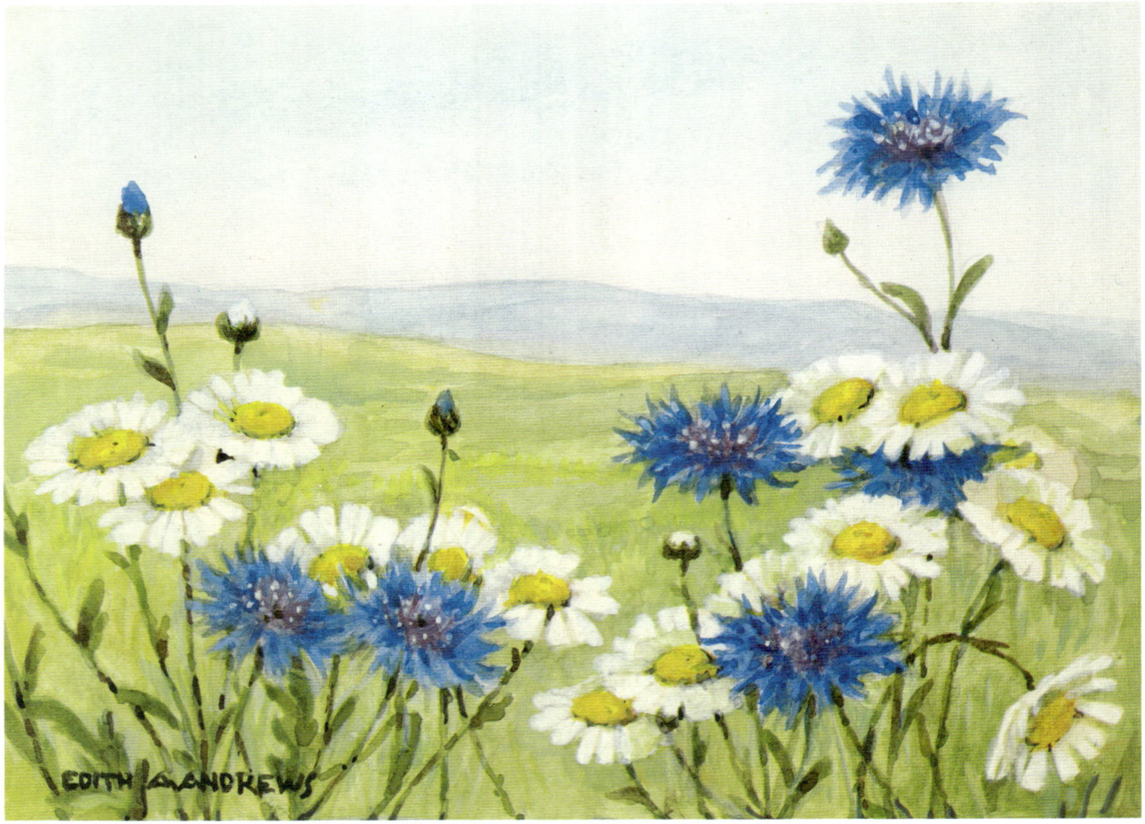

Flowers of the Field by Edith A Andrews

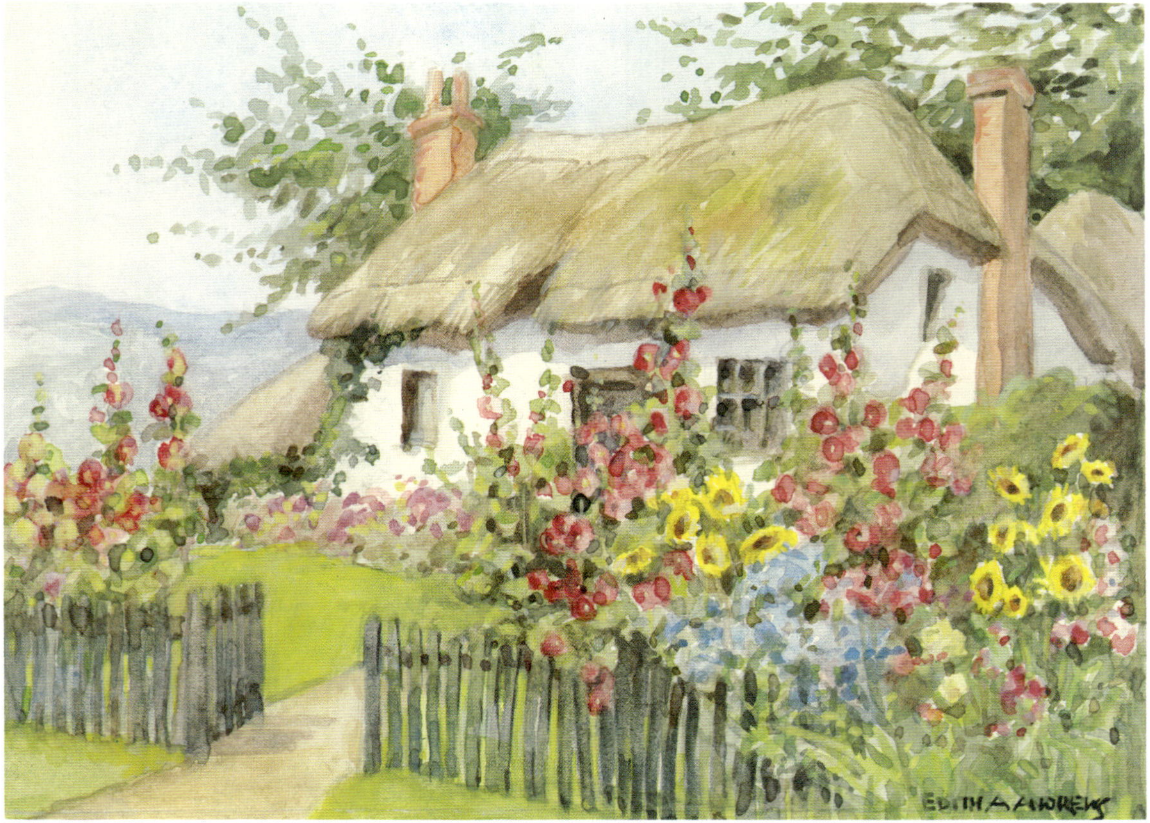

Hollyhock Cottage by Edith A Andrews

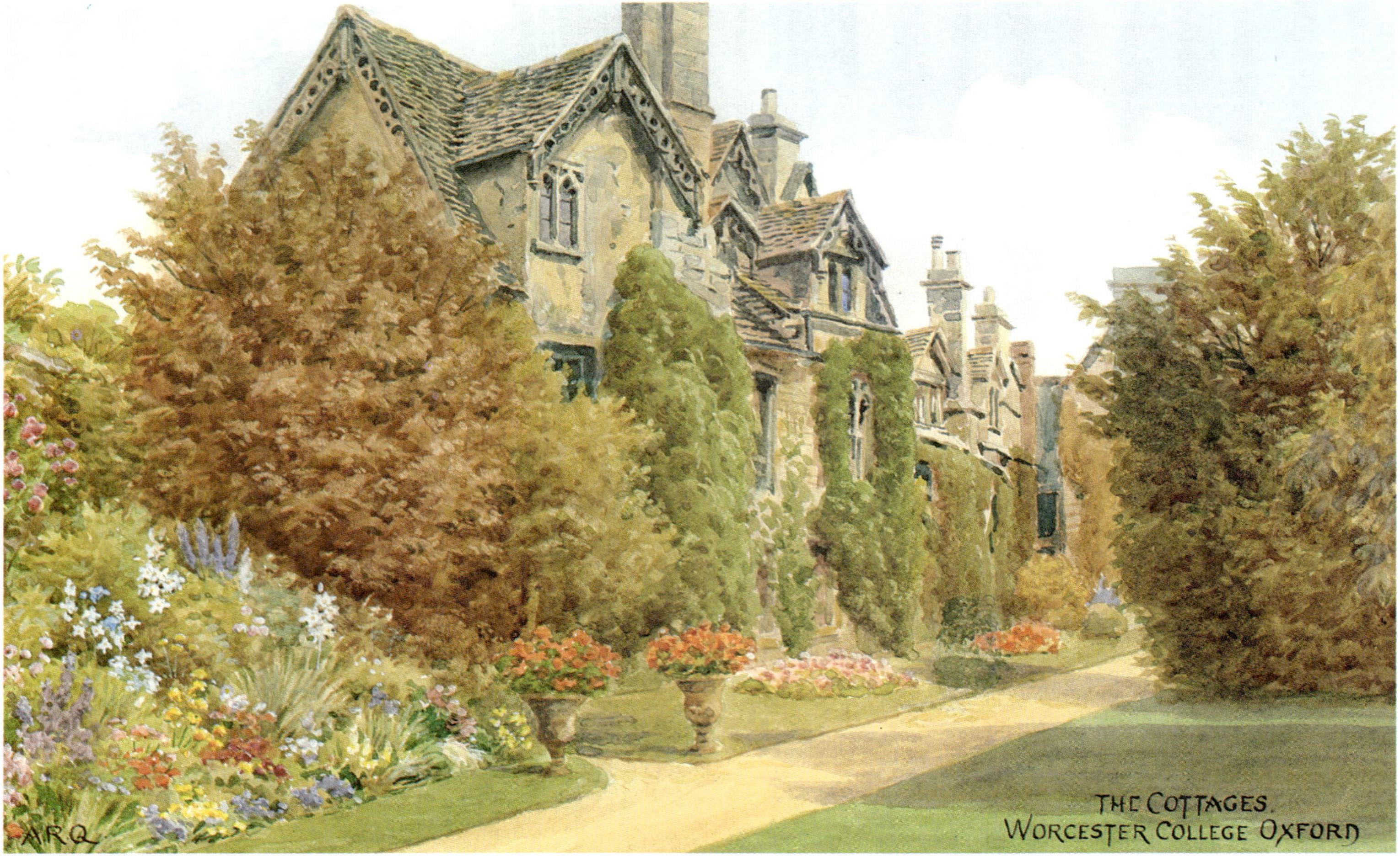

The Cottage, Worcester College, Oxford by A R Quinton

ALFRED ROBERT QUINTON was a watercolour painter of English landscapes and cottages. He was born on 23rd October 1853, the youngest of seven children of John and Eliza Quinton. He attended Hornsey School in North London and after studying at Heatherley's Art School started work as an engraver, but he soon took up painting seriously. From 1874 onwards Quinton was a regular exhibitor at various London societies and galleries and he first exhibited at the Royal Academy in 1879. Many of his watercolours were used as illustrations in magazines, books and on post cards. In his paintings Quinton's particular gift was his ability to capture the flavour and colour of rural England at the turn of the century. He lived at Finchley, North London and died in 1934.

Gathering Bluebells
by Howard Walford

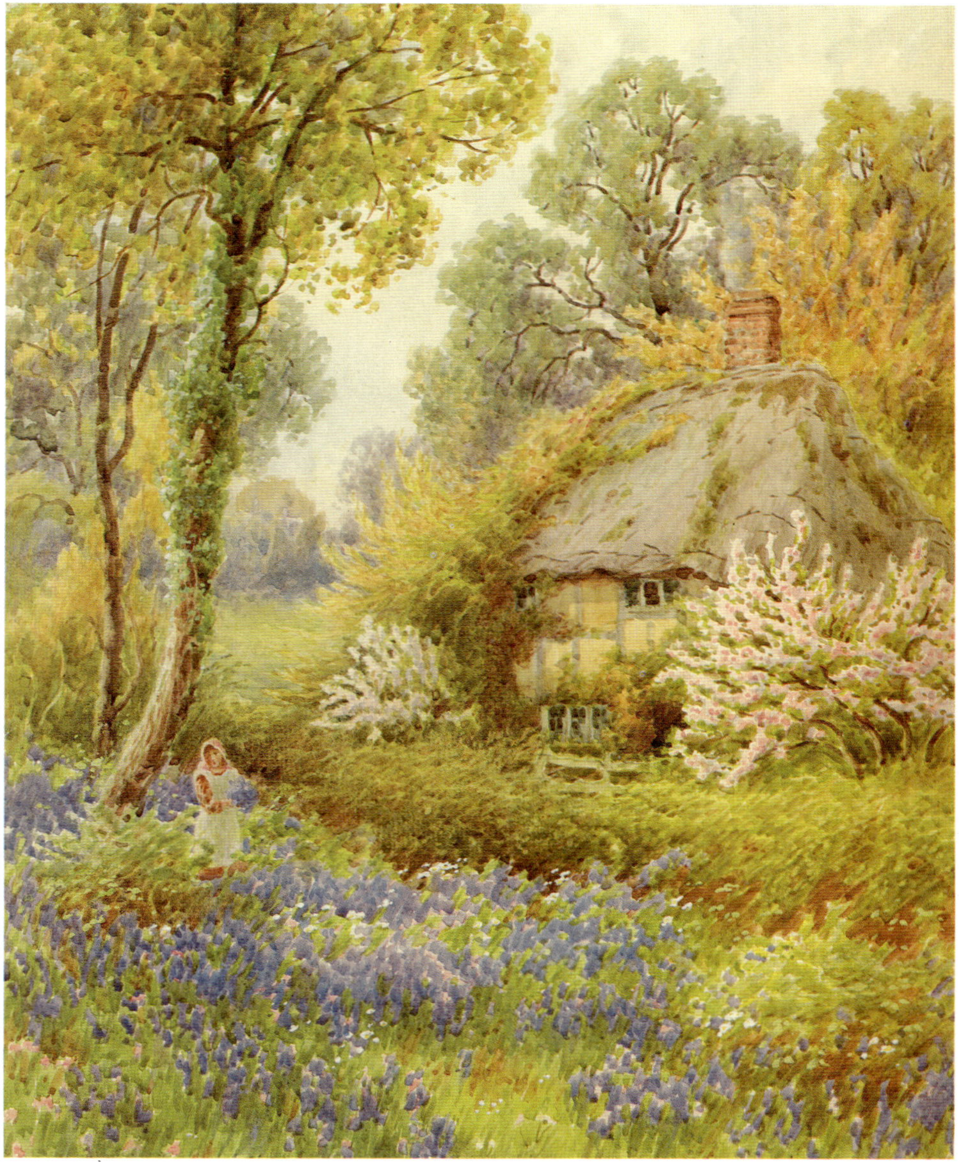

NOVEMBER

When the leaves have fallen collect and put them into a good deep heap to form leaf soil or hot beds. Give the lawn a thorough hard sweeping; if in poor shape a dressing with a sward restorer will work wonders. Plant up any new shrubs, climbers or roses; for the roses work in plenty of good manure into the soil; they are heavy feeders. As the herbacious plants die down cut off the tall rough shoots; not too close, always leave a foot or two of the old stems for protection. Rearrange and thoroughly dig the borders every three or four years. Finish fruit picking and start pruning; try and get as much done as you can before the severe frosts. Spray with a tar-oil wash every two or three years, thoroughly wetting every twig from base to summit. Give the Strawberry bed a clean over, lightly forking the soil and drawing the soil well up to the plants. Cut over the old Asparagus growths, clean and manure the beds – about four inches of well-rotted manure right over the crowns – and cover with a little soil from the alleys; leave it rough as it falls from the spade. Plan your crops for next year and dig and manure accordingly.

Autumn Glory by A de Breanski Jnr

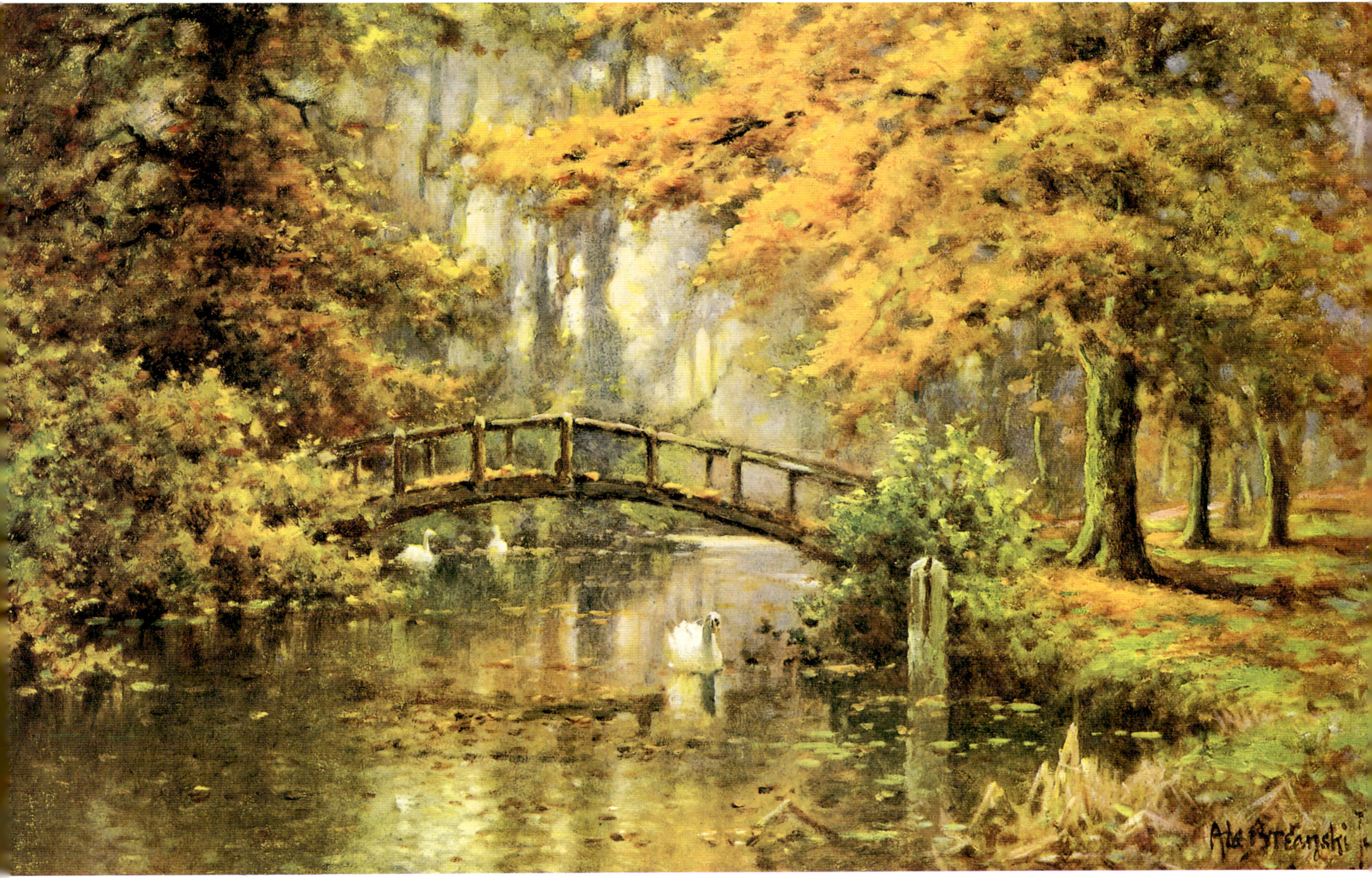

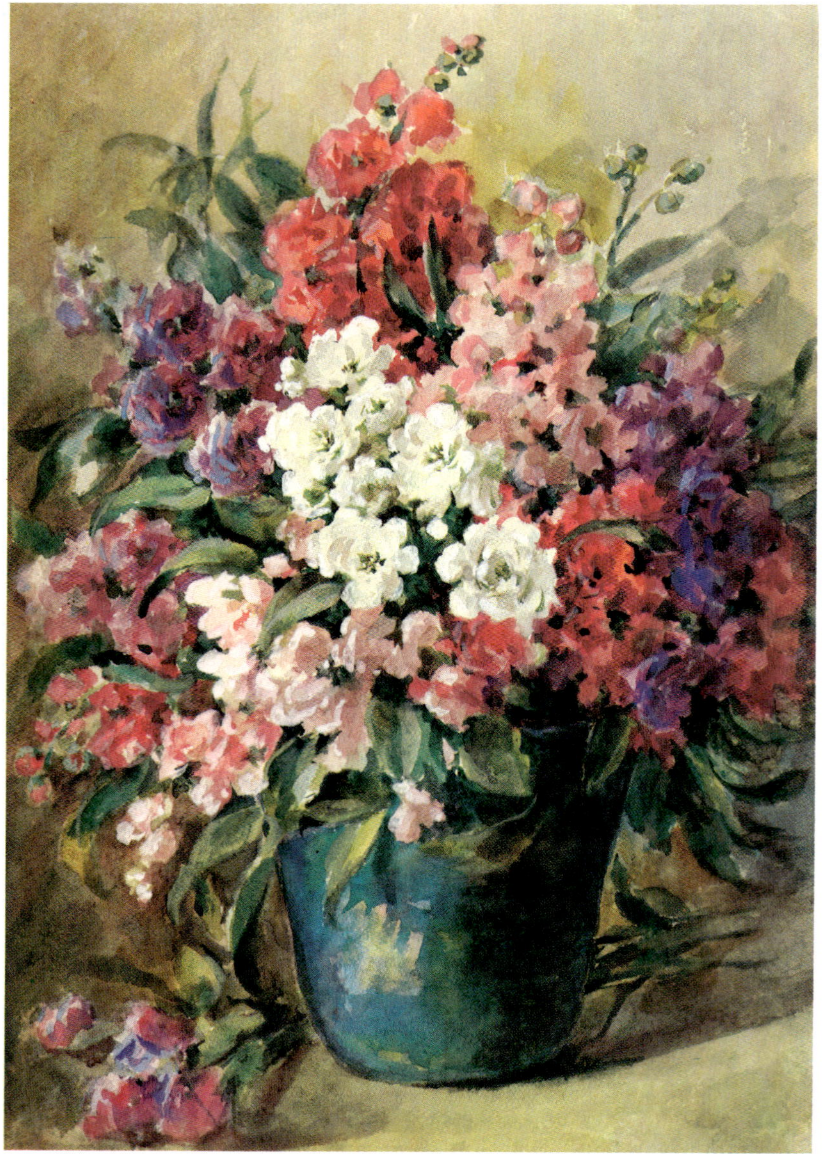

ALFRED FONTVILLE DE BREANSKI was a painter of landscapes, highland scenes and gardens, mainly in oil. He was born in 1877, the son of Alfred de Breanski (1852-1928) also a landscape painter in oils and a nephew of Gustave de Breanski, a painter of landscapes and more especially coastal scenes. Alfred Junior painted with a strong, rich pallette in a style somewhat similar to that of his father with whom his work is sometimes confused, but with a coarser texture and broader handling of the medium; he exhibited at the Royal Academy. He lived at the Old Ferry House, Chalmore near Wallingford, Berkshire later moving to Tunbridge Wells, Kent where he died in 1951.

Stocks by Annie L Pressland

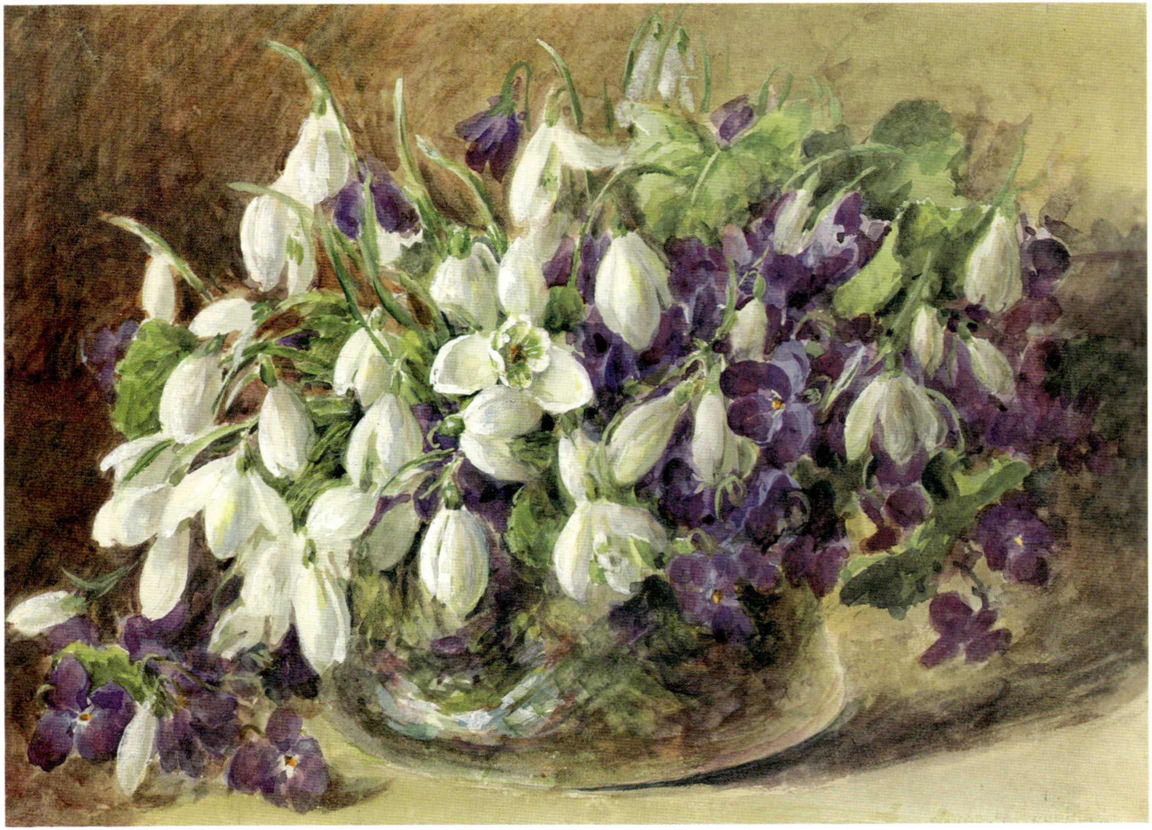

Snowdrops and Violets by Annie L Pressland

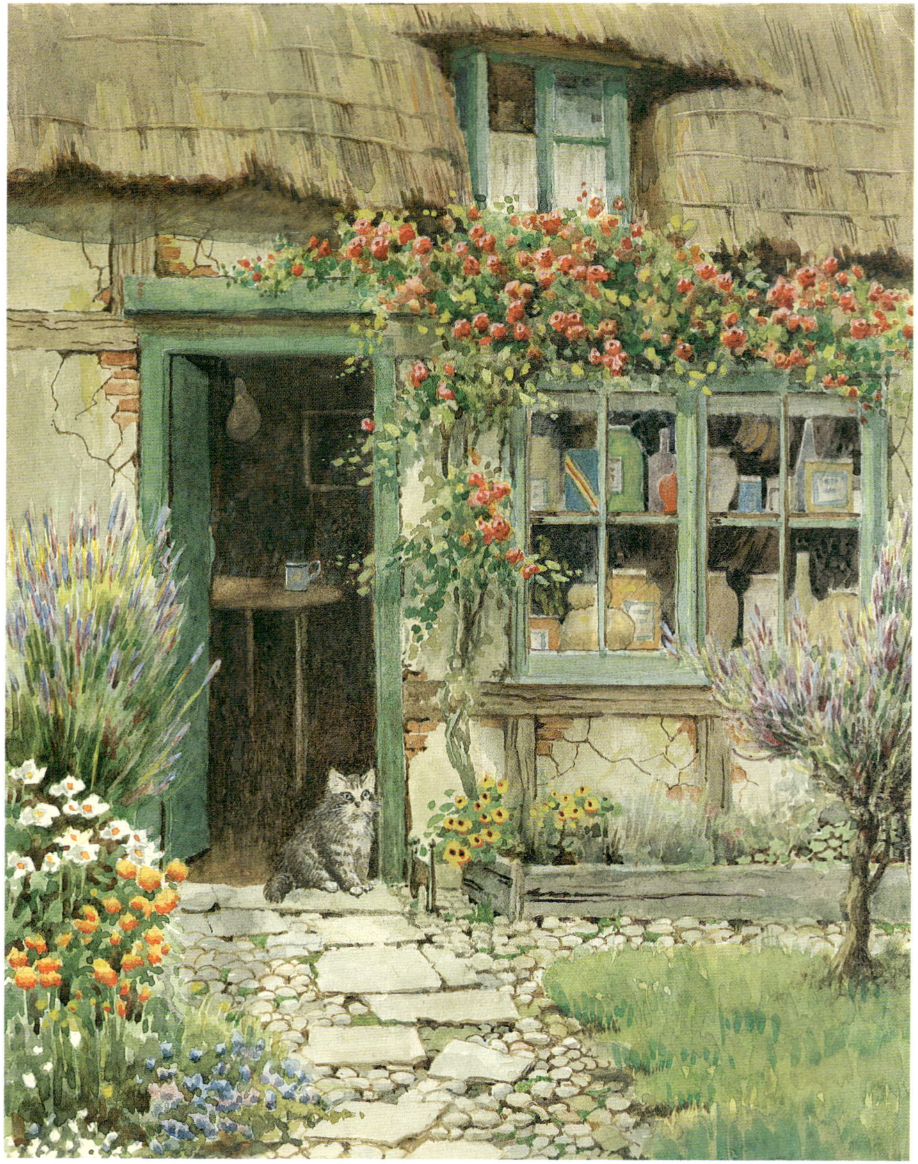

Pleasures lie thickest where no
pleasures seem;
There's not a leaf that falls upon
the ground
But holds some joy of silence or
of sound,
Some sprite begotten of a summer
dream.

Laman Blanchard

The Village Shop
by William F Ashburner

Autumn to winter, winter into
    spring,
Spring into summer, summer
    into fall, –
So rolls the changing year, and so we
    change;
Motion so swift, we know not that
    we move.

D M Mulock

The Courtyard
by William F Ashburner

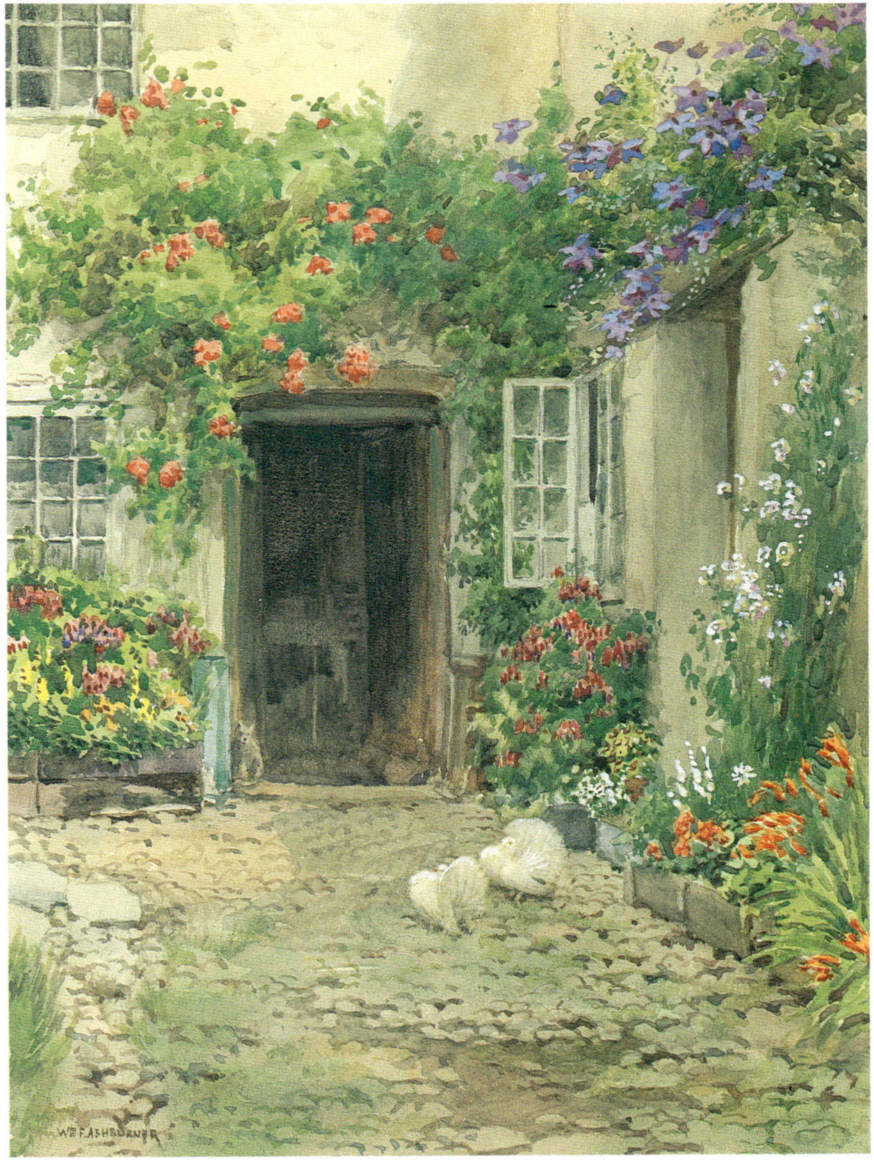

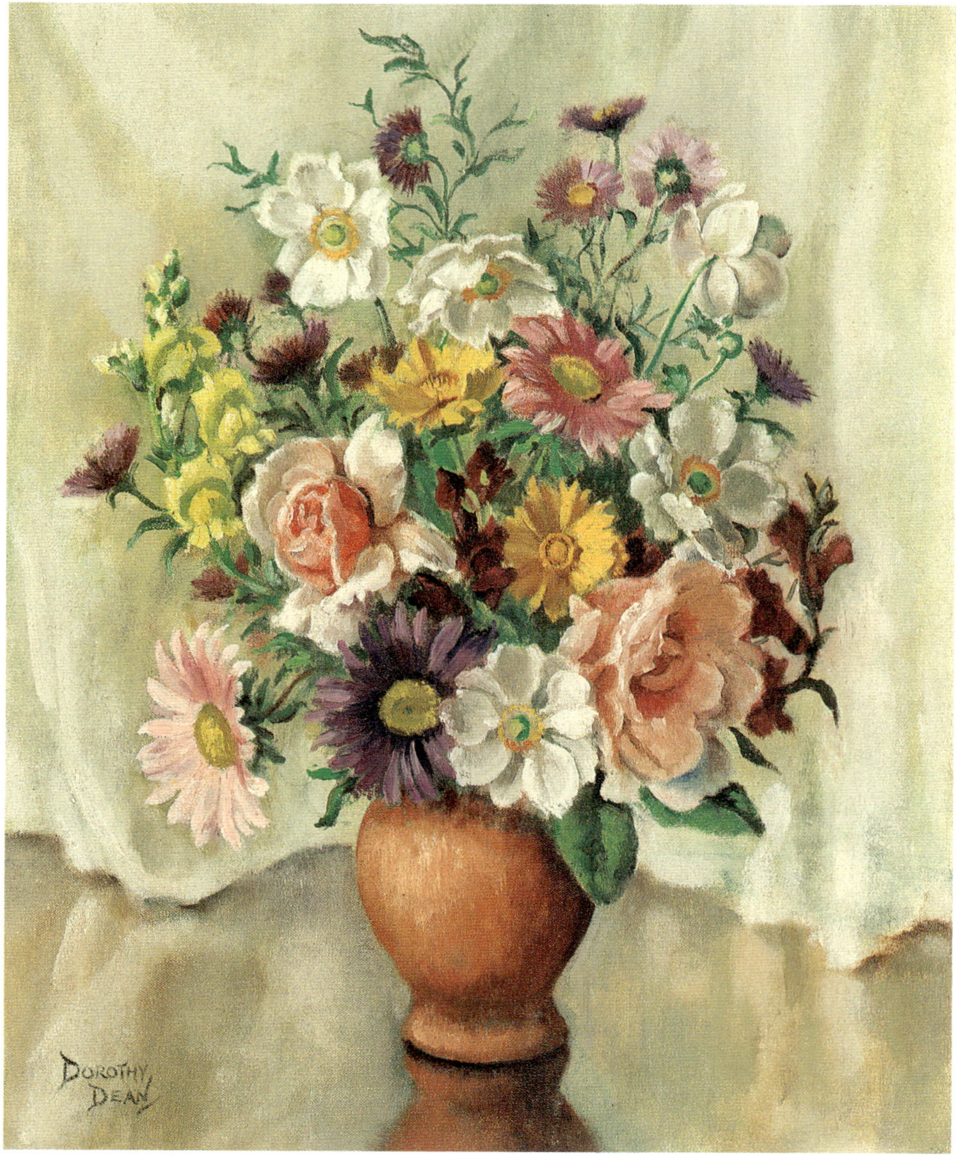

Flowers have an expression of countenance as much as men or animals. Some seem to smile; some have a sad expression; some are pensive and diffident; others again are plain, honest and upright, like the broad-faced sunflower and the hollyhock.

Henry Ward Beecher

Summer Harvest by Dorothy Dean

Where grows? – where grows it
not? If vain our toil,
We ought to blame the culture, not
the soil.

Alexander Pope

Mixed Summer Flowers
by Nora H Cullen

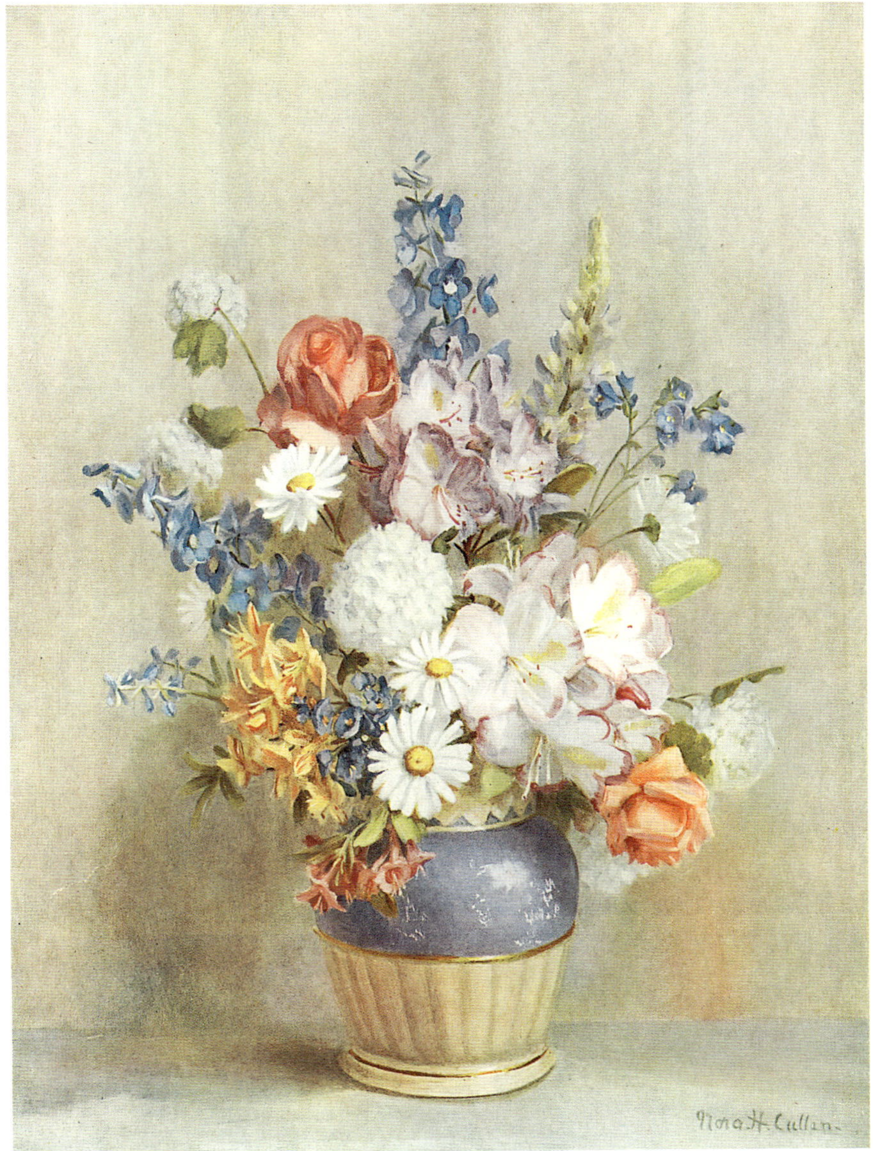

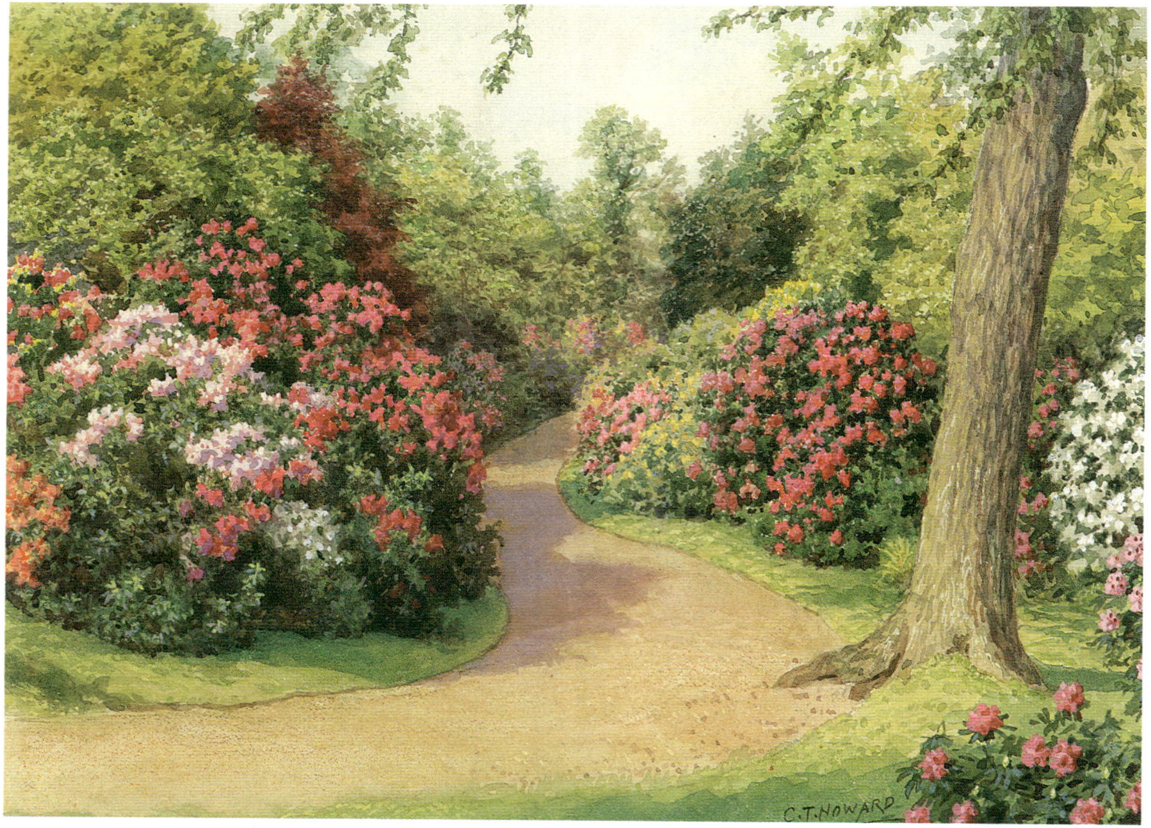

The Rhododendron Walk, Kew Gardens by C T Howard

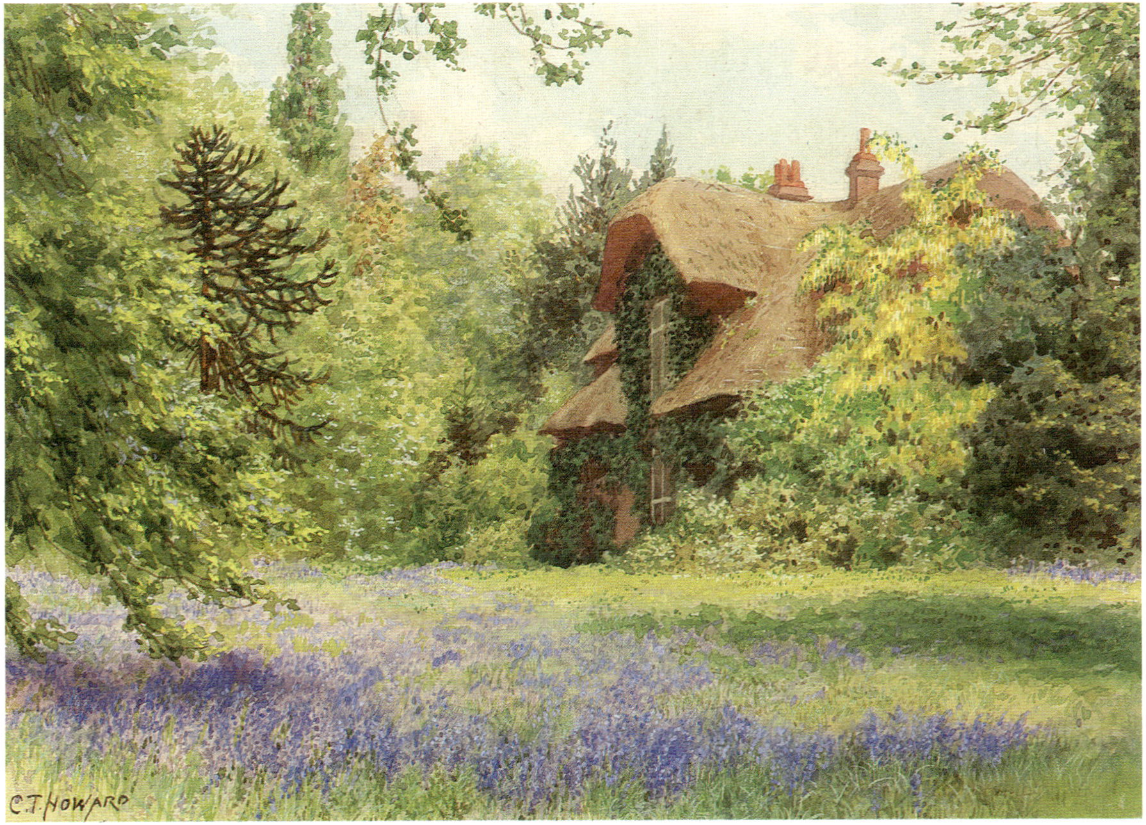

The Queen's Cottage, Kew Gardens by C T Howard

DECEMBER

Push on with the clearing up in all parts of the garden as the weather permits. Remove all yellow leaves from your Brussels Sprouts and Winter Greens; leave your latish varieties till last. Deeply dig your Onion bed, Pea and Bean ground and give them as much manure as you can spare, but plain digging for root crops. Always leave the surface as rough as possible and lime 8 ozs to the square yard, if needed. Watch your Potatoes in store; not a bad plan to go over them when outside work is impossible. Keep a sharp look out for vermin. Bring the Christmas bulbs in the first week, remove the others from the covering into a frame and keep them cool. Still time to plant bulbs. See that the plants in the house are kept watered well at Christmas time, never let them get dry. Keep your Autumn-sown Sweet Peas as cool as you can. Try to finish pruning and spraying by Christmas Day, except Gooseberries and Red Currants, and get the place real smart and clean.

A Cottage Garden in Suffolk by Edith A Andrews

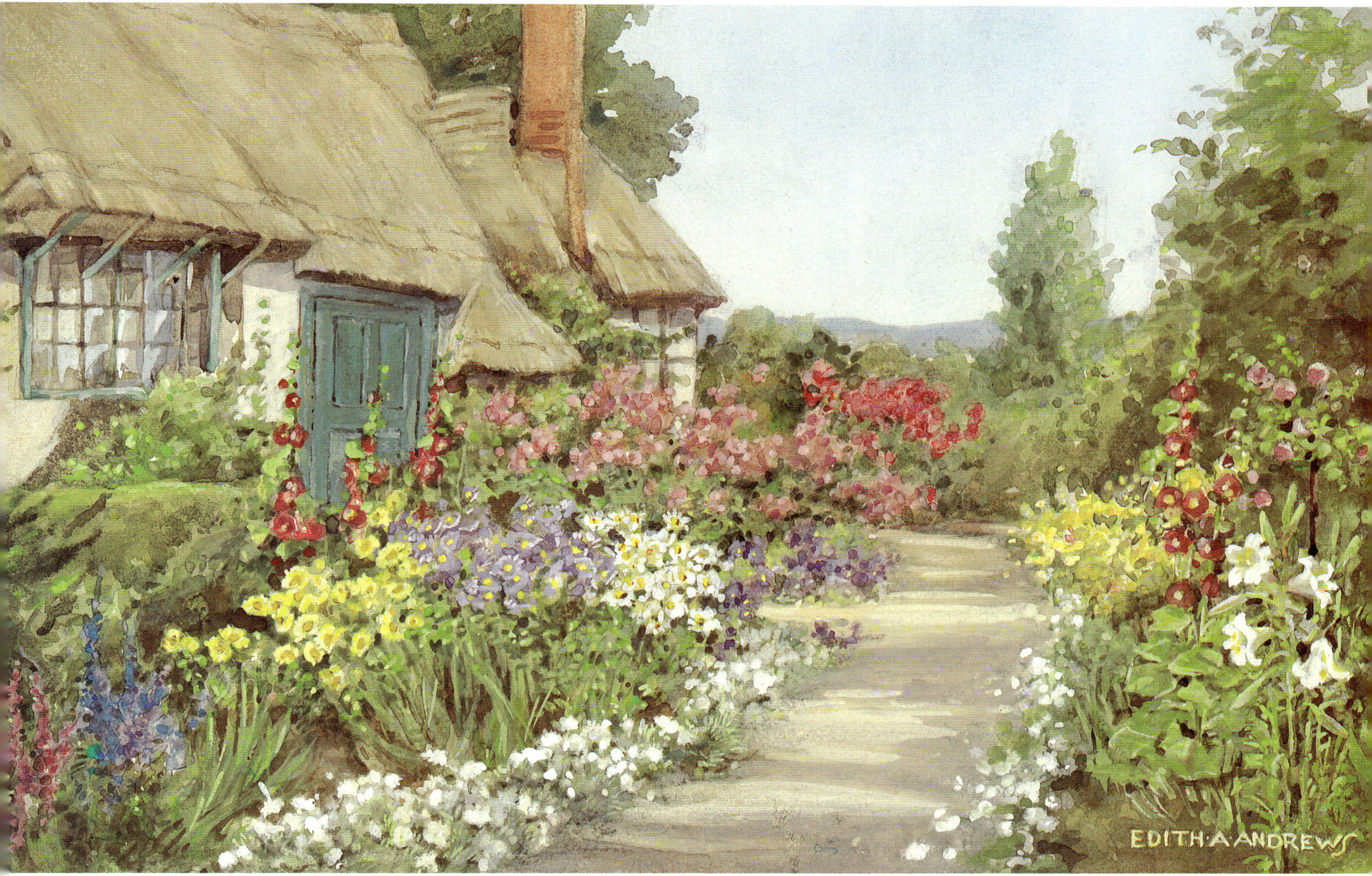
EDITH A ANDREWS

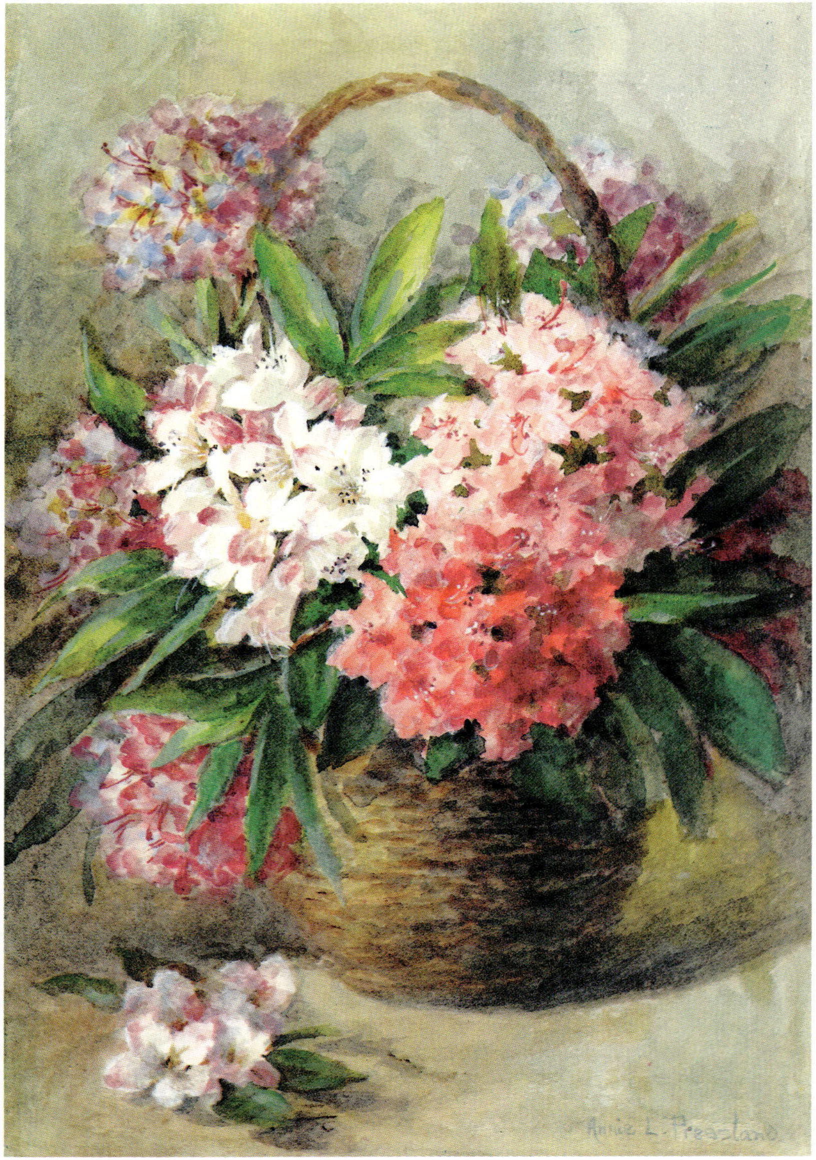

Go, little book, and wish to all
Flowers in the garden, meat
 in the hall,
A bin of wine, a spice of wit,
A house with lawns enclosing it,
A living river by the door,
A nightingale in the sycamore.
Robert Louis Stevenson

Rhododendrons
by Annie L Pressland

WILLIAM WELLS QUATREMAIN was a watercolour artist who spent his entire life painting scenes in and around his home town of Stratford-upon-Avon. He also painted stage sets for the Shakespeare Memorial Theatre. He was born on 22nd December 1857 to William Jarrett Quatremain and his wife Elizabeth. After his father's death ten years later, mother and son lived together in Stratford until her death in 1892 when he was aged 34. In 1895 he married a widow, Eliza Marshall, five years his senior. Quatremain appears to have been self-taught but by 1903 he was an established artist and for the next 30 years he spent his time recording Stratford. He was a shy man who had an aversion to art galleries and dealers and sold many of his pictures through his wife's confectionery and art shop. He died in March 1930.

Larkspur by Annie L Pressland

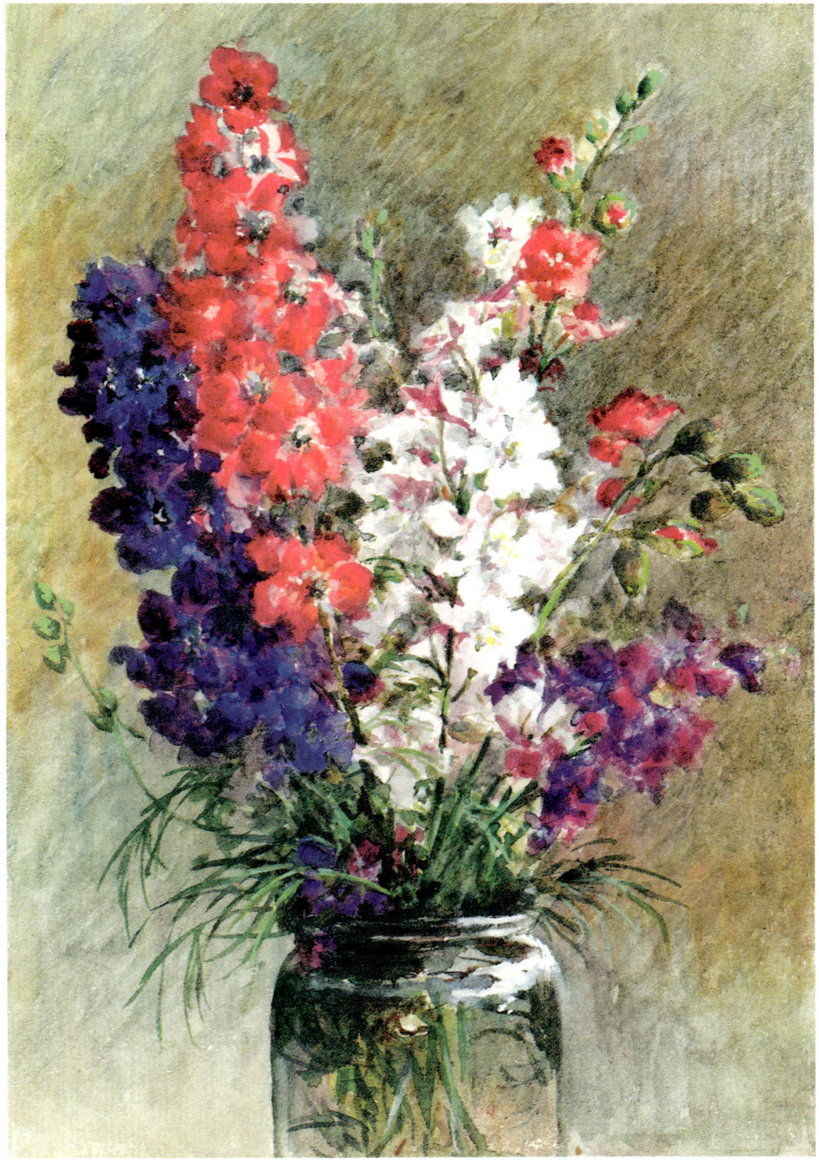

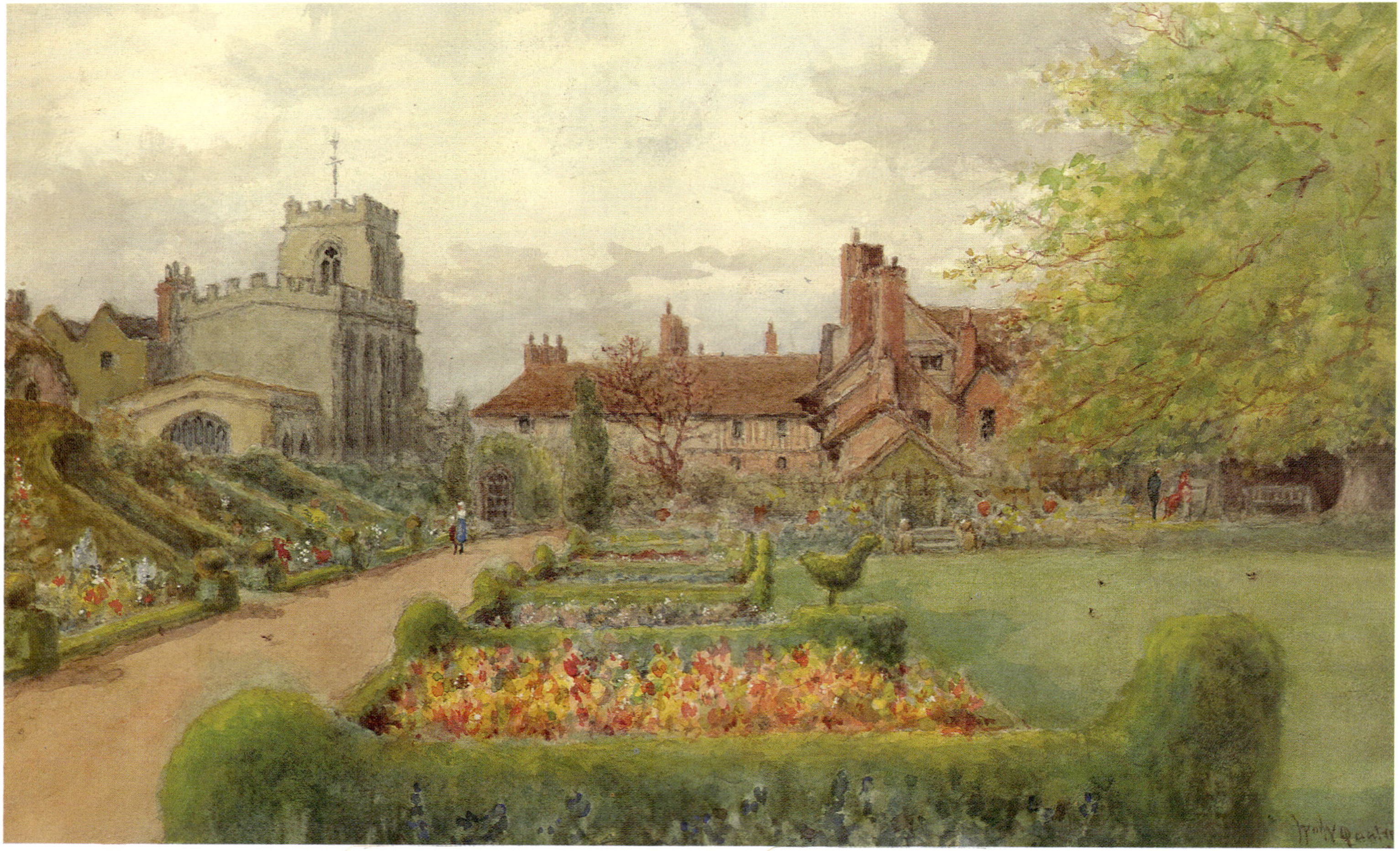

The Great Garden, New Place, Stratford-upon-Avon by W W Quatremain

I know a bank whereon the wild
thyme blows,
Where oxlips and the nodding
violet grows
Quite over canopied with luscious
woodbine,
With sweet musk-roses and with
eglantine.

William Shakespeare

Anne Hathaway's Cottage
by Florence F Wilmot

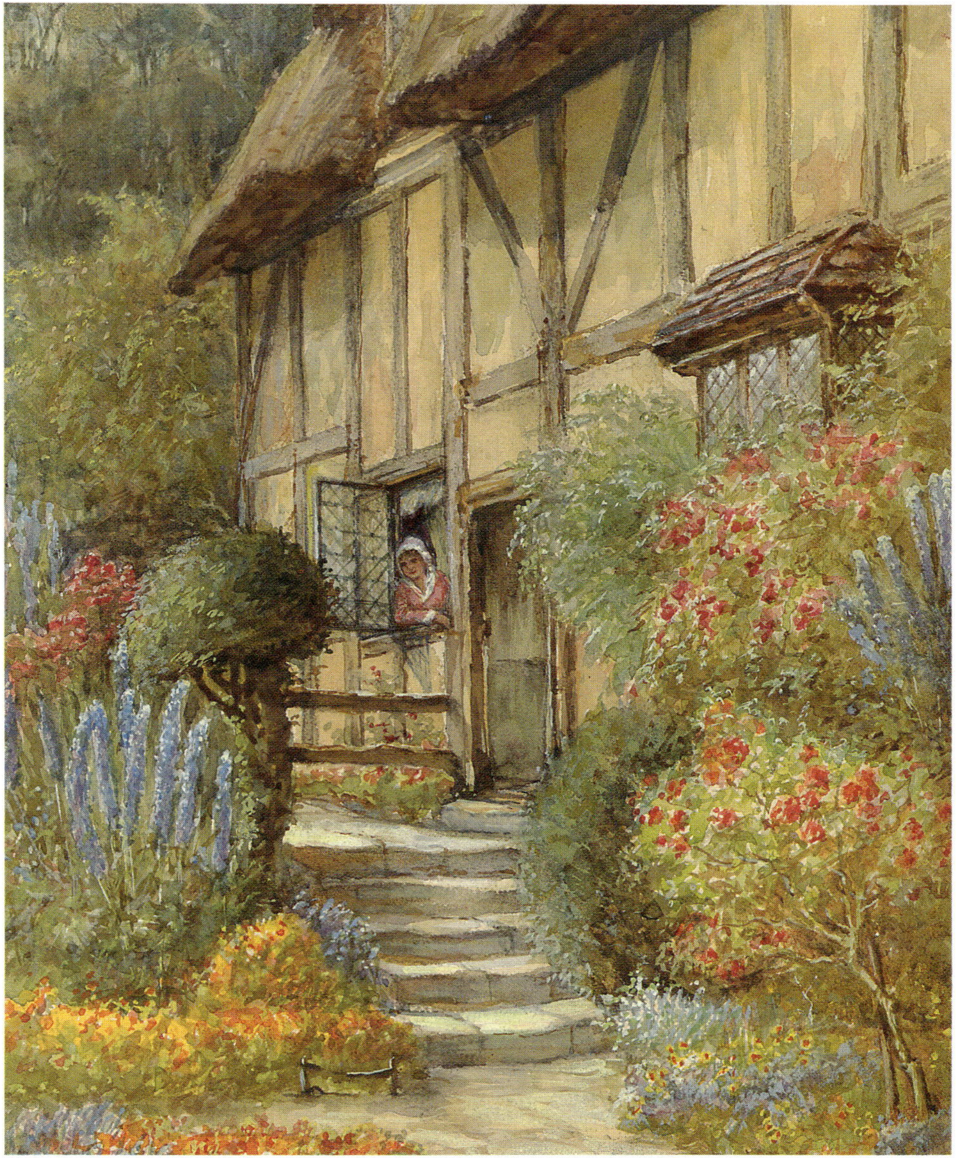

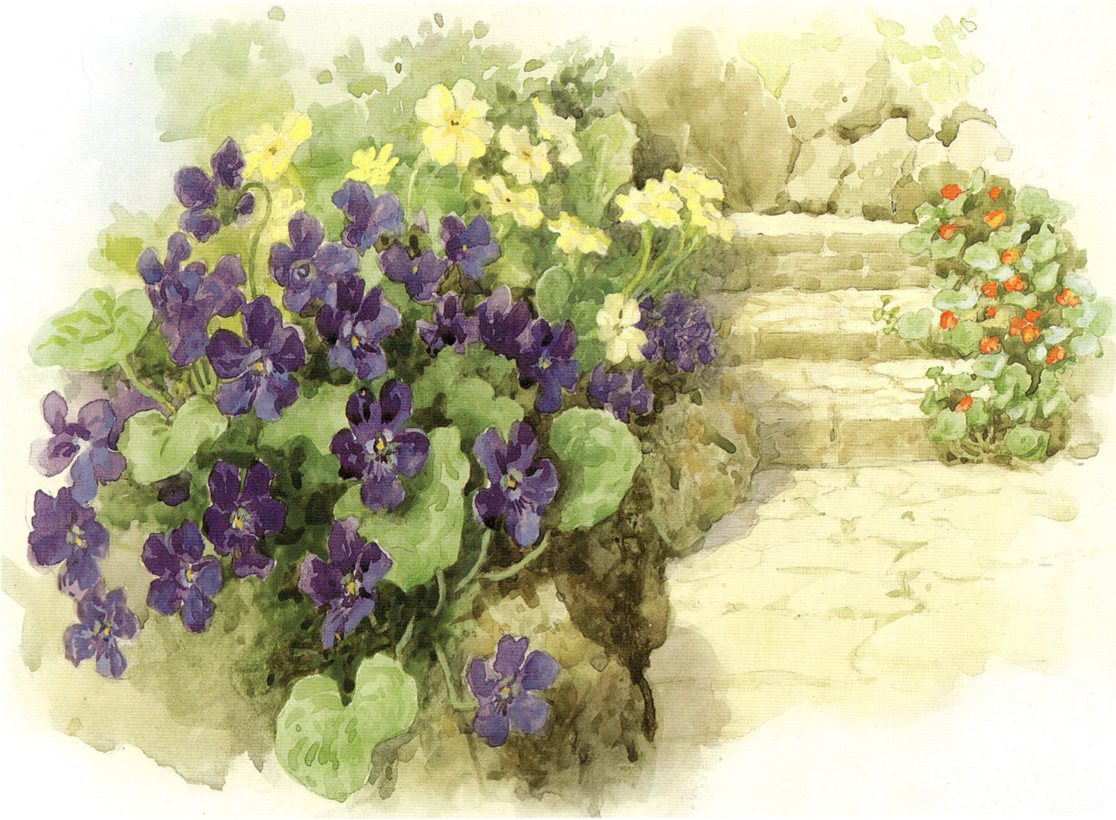

Violets and Primroses by C T Howard